An Annotated Checklist of Peruvian Birds

An Annotated Checklist
of
Peruvian Birds

by

Theodore A. Parker III
Susan Allen Parker
Manuel A. Plenge

Cover Illustration of Long-whiskered Owlet by John P. O'Neill

BUTEO BOOKS
Vermillion, South Dakota

First published in 1982 by Buteo Books, PO Box 481,
Vermillion, South Dakota 57069.

Library of Congress Catalog Card Number 81-66046
ISBN 0-931130-07-7

Printed in the United States of America by
North Central Publishing Company, St. Paul, Minnesota.

Peruvian Booby (*Sula variegata*) and young, Isla Lobos de Tierra, Dpto. Lambayeque, 15 July 1978. Photo by M. D. Williams.

CONTENTS

MAPS

INTRODUCTION

Peru has an amazingly diverse avifauna, with new species discovered nearly every year in its Andean cloud forests and Amazonian lowlands. The geography of the country is spectacular, encompassing an astonishing variety of habitats, ranging from coastal deserts to vast expanses of tropical rainforest. Between these extremes are dry forests, high-elevation grasslands, and cloud forests of indescribable beauty.

In this publication we list 1678 species of birds recorded in Peru as of 31 December 1980, and give some indication of their elevational distribution, relative abundance, and habitat preference. We also briefly describe and illustrate the life zones and major habitats of the country. A section on bird-finding is included as an introduction to some of the better and more accessible areas for birdwatching in the country. At the end we provide a useful list of references and indexes to both the common names and the genera of species included in the list.

Until recently the lack of good field guides discouraged many birdwatchers from travelling to most South American countries. Though there is still no comprehensive book on Peruvian birds, several excellent guides for other countries are very helpful in Peru. The best of these is *A Guide to the Birds of Venezuela* (Meyer de Schauensee and Phelps 1978), which is especially useful for identifying humid montane and lowland forest birds in Peru. *The Birds of the Department of Lima* (Koepcke 1970) and *The Birds of Chile and Adjacent Regions of Argentina, Bolivia and Peru* (Johnson 1965, 1967, and 1972) describe and illustrate most of the birds of the coast and drier parts of the Andes. These first three books are also available in Spanish editions (Phelps and Meyer de Schauensee 1979, Koepcke 1964, and Goodall, Johnson, and Phillipi 1946 and 1951; 1957 and 1964). Finally, *A Guide to the Birds of South America* (Meyer de Schauensee 1970) describes and gives the distributions of nearly all species found in Peru, but its illustrations are not very useful and it can be difficult to use unless the observer is familiar with the pertinent families and, especially, genera. Two excellent guides are forthcoming: *A Guide to the Birds of Colombia* (Hilty and Brown, MS) and *A Guide to the Birds of the Paracas Peninsula Region* (O'Neill and Plenge, MS). In addition to the above references we advise interested readers to familiarize themselves with locality lists provided in several recent articles: Parker and O'Neill (1976a,b and 1981), Donahue *et al.* (MS), O'Neill and Pearson (1974), and Terborgh (MS).

We gratefully acknowledge the assistance of the many friends who contributed to the production of this list. We especially appreciate the constant encouragement of John P. O'Neill, and also his gracious permission to use the beautiful plate of the Long-whiskered Owlet as our cover illustration. Isabel Plenge was unfailing in her support of the project. The fieldwork that has been conducted in Peru by a number of Peruvian, North American and European scientists has contributed immeasurably to the compilation of an accurate listing of the birds in the country. We would particularly like to mention the ongoing field expeditions sponsored by the Louisiana State University Museum of Zoology. Any proceeds we receive from the sale of this publication will go directly into the LSU Peruvian Expedition Fund, in order to assist in the perpetuation of ornithological investigations in Peru. A factor in making the field expeditions possible has been the kind assistance and interest in our work on the part of Antonio Brack E., Eric Cardich B., Marc Dourojeanni R., Susana Moller H., Carlos Ponce P., and José Purisaca P. of the Dirección General Forestal y de Fauna of the Ministry of Agriculture, Lima, Peru. We are grateful for the painstaking review of our various drafts of this list by Thomas S. Schulenberg and Douglas F. Stotz. We also thank John Farrand, Jr., John W. Fitzpatrick, Robin A. Hughes and Guy Tudor for commenting on the manuscript, and Alwyn Gentry for his critique of the habitat descriptions. Norman and Maggie Mellor kindly provided us with a first draft of the index to common names, and Thomas Y. Butler generously allowed us to adapt the format of his Ecuador list (Butler 1979).

Finally, special thanks are due Helen and Arturo Koenig of Lima and Gustavo del Solar R. of Chiclayo, who have assisted us in ways too numerous to mention during our many years of research in Peru. Although many people have given financial assistance toward the LSUMZ field work in Peru, we must give special recognition to John S. McIlhenny and Babette M. Odom for their unequaled and continued interest.

We hope that this annotated checklist will enable readers to prepare themselves for birding or fieldwork in Peru. Any comments or suggestions from people who use this list will be greatly appreciated. Please feel free to write to any of us.

Theodore A. Parker III	Susan Allen Parker	Manuel A. Plenge
Museum of Zoology	Museum of Zoology	Casilla 2490
Louisiana State University	Louisiana State University	Lima 100
Baton Rouge, LA 70893	Baton Rouge, LA 70893	Peru

TAXONOMY

We have used a variety of taxonomic sources in compiling this list. For those species that occur within the A.O.U. Check-list area we use as prime authority the American Ornithologists' Union *Check-list of North American Birds*, 5th ed. (1957) and its supplements (1973, 1976). For the Cracidae we follow Delacour and Amadon (1973). For flycatchers, manakins and cotingas we use the *Check-list of Birds of the World*, Vol. 8 (Traylor 1979). The authority for all remaining families is *The Species of Birds of South America* (Meyer de Schauensee 1966). Three other important works (Blake 1977, Morony *et al.* 1975, and Paynter 1970) were referred to extensively, particularly where field or museum experience suggested that the taxonomic treatment of our main authority might be inadequate. In several instances, particularly for poorly known or recently described species, we have relied on the judgment of persons familiar with the species in question.

The following is a list of those species that appear in our checklist but are not mentioned in one of our major sources (i.e. Meyer de Schauensee 1966, 1970). After each species listed below is either an explanation for its inclusion or a reference, usually referring to the original description of the species.

Broad-billed Prion *Pachyptila vittata* — details forthcoming
Medium-billed Prion *Pachyptila salvini* — details forthcoming
Rock Dove *Columba livia* — introduced
Otus sp. nov. — description forthcoming
Otus sp. nov. — description forthcoming

Cloud-forest Screech-Owl *Otus marshalli* — Weske and Terborgh 1981
Long-whiskered Owlet *Xenoglaux loweryi* — O'Neill and Graves 1977
Koepcke's Hermit *Phaethornis koepckeae* — Weske and Terborgh 1977
Royal Sunangel *Heliangelus regalis* — Fitzpatrick, Willard, and Terborgh 1979
Neblina Metaltail *Metallura odomae* — Graves 1980
Purus Jacamar *Galbalcyrhynchus purusianus* — Haffer 1974
Blue-cheeked Jacamar *Galbula cyanicollis* — Haffer 1974
Marcapata Piculet *Picumnus subtilis* — Stager 1968
Elegant Spinetail *Synallaxis elegantior* — Vaurie 1971
Coursen's Spinetail *Synallaxis courseni* — Blake 1971
Chapman's Antshrike *Thamnophilus zarumae* — Chapman 1921
Marcapata Antshrike *Thamnophilus marcapatae* — Short 1975
Cercomacra sp. nov. — description forthcoming
White-lined Antbird *Percnostola lophotes* = *Percnostola macrolopha* — details forthcoming; these were found in 1977 to be male and female of the same species
Grallaria sp. nov. — description forthcoming
Grallaricula sp. nov. — description forthcoming
Poecilotriccus sp. nov. — description forthcoming
Cinnamon-breasted Tody-Tyrant *Hemitriccus cinnamomeipectus* — Fitzpatrick and O'Neill 1979
Thryothorus sp. nov. — description forthcoming
Bar-winged Wood-Wren *Henicorhina leucoptera* — Fitzpatrick, Terborgh, and Willard 1977
Tamarugo Conebill *Conirostrum tamarugensis* — Johnson and Millie 1972
Black-throated Flower-piercer *Diglossa brunneiventris* — Graves (in press)
O'Neill's Pardusco *Nephelornis oneilli* — Lowery and Tallman 1976
Golden-backed Mountain-Tanager *Buthraupis aureodorsalis* — Blake and Hocking 1974
Orange-browed Hemispingus *Hemispingus calophrys* — Weske and Terborgh 1974
Parodi's Hemispingus *Hemispingus parodii* — Weske and Terborgh 1974
Rufous-browed Hemispingus *Hemispingus rufosuperciliaris* — Blake and Hocking 1974

EXPLANATION OF ANNOTATIONS

There are several symbols used throughout the list that have taxonomic significance. Indentation of a species' name indicates some controversy in its taxonomic status. Included in this list are most recognizable forms that either have been or could be considered full species. To indicate those forms that are considered specifically distinct by Meyer de Schauensee (1966) but that we or others feel should be recognized as forms of another species we have used a dagger (*e.g.*, Silver Teal and Puna Teal). Those indented species without a dagger are recognizable forms of uncertain specific status. Refer to Meyer de Schauensee (1966) for an explanation of many of these cases. The presence of a line for recording information indicates that a species is found in Peru. Occasionally only forms other than the nominate one occur in Peru (*e.g.*, Lesser Rhea and Puna Rhea); in these cases we also include the nominate form but we omit the line for it. An asterisk indicates a species known only from a sight record, for which there is as yet no specimen for Peru.

The checklist also contains symbols that provide information on relative abundance, distribution within life zones, and preferred habitats. The vertical columns represent the life zones one would encounter while travelling from the Pacific coast east across Peru to the Brazilian border. Symbols within the columns represent relative abundance. Numbers to the far right of each page indicate a species' preferred habitat within the life zones where it occurs. The task of assigning the variety of annotations to each species was quite difficult, due largely to a lack of information in many cases. The avifauna of Peru is relatively poorly known, and any astute observer has an opportunity to add considerably to the knowledge of birds in the country. All symbols contained in the list are explained below.

Status

Symbols of relative abundance are provided to give an idea of which species might be encountered during a given time in a given habitat. Abundances of some species differ from place to place and from season to season, but we try to give our impression of what is 'normal' based on extensive fieldwork throughout the country. The following symbols reflect relative abundance within a species' preferred habitat.

      C = Common; seen or heard daily in moderate to large numbers.
      F = Fairly common; seen or heard daily in small numbers.
      U = Uncommon; seen or heard on one out of three days; occurs in small numbers.
      R = Rare; seen or heard on one out of six days or less often; occurs in small numbers.

The following designations may be combined with one of the above symbols:

      n = north; species occurs in northern third of the country. Many of these species do not range south of the Marañón River. When this designation is used in the Arid Tropical Zone, the implication is that the species does not range south of Tumbes or Piura.

      c = central; species occurs in the central portion of the country (e.g., Huánuco and Junín). When this designation is used in the Arid Tropical Zone, the implication is that the species is found in the arid Marañón River valley.

s = south; the species is restricted to the southern third of the country.

l = local; a species may be absent from seemingly suitable habitat, though it may be common where it does occur, or is found in patchily-distributed habitats (*e.g.*, bamboo thickets). Also included here are wandering, often sporadically common species such as *Sporophila* seedeaters.

m = migrant; species occurs in Peru only at certain seasons, migrating from some other region. Many pelagic seabirds breed on south Pacific islands and in the Antarctic, moving northward during the austral winter months of June to August. Other seabirds that breed in the Galápagos Islands are found in Peruvian waters during their non-breeding season. Migrant and wintering shorebirds from North America can be expected throughout the year, but are most common from August to May. Relatively few Nearctic landbirds migrate as far south as Peru; most of these appear in October and depart by early April. Austral migrants, both shorebirds and landbirds, are found mostly from May to September.

i = introduced

? = status uncertain

Life Zones

The life zones, as read from left to right, represent very generally a transect from the coast, across the two Andean ranges, to the lowland forest in eastern Peru. The following figure is of a hypothetical east-west transect, superimposed on the life zone categories that we use.

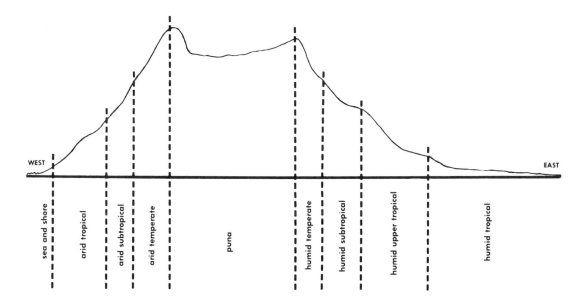

The names of the life zones are adapted from those used by Chapman (1926) in his study of Ecuadorean birds. Readers interested in understanding the factors that determine elevational distribution of birds in the Andes should refer to Terborgh and Weske (1975).

Map 1. The Life Zones of Peru.

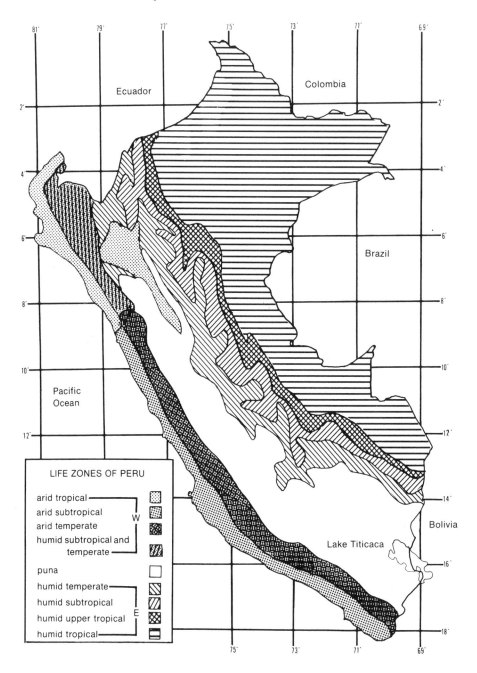

Map by Susan Parker, modified from "Provincias Bioticas del Peru" by Dr. A. Brack Egg (MS)

Each life zone is described below with regard to climate and elevation. The place names, unless otherwise designated, refer to the 24 departments of Peru, which are administrative subdivisions equivalent to states or provinces.

Sea and Shore — includes sea, shore, and coastal marshes from Tumbes to Tacna, and mangroves in the far north.

Arid Tropical — coastal lowlands and lower slopes of the Andes from Tumbes south to La Libertad, and also dry parts of the Marañón, Apurímac, Éne, and Urubamba River valleys. Elevation is sea level to 1500 m (5000 ft).

Arid Subtropical — coastal lowlands and west slope of the Western Andes from Ancash to Tacna, and slopes of dry intermontane valleys throughout the country. Elevation is sea level to 2500 m (8000 ft).

Arid Temperate — west slope of the Western Andes from Ancash to Tacna, and slopes of dry intermontane valleys. Elevation is 2500 to 3400 m (8000 to 11,000 ft).

Humid Subtropical and Temperate — west slope of the Western Andes from Piura to Lima; only isolated relict forests of this life zone occur south of Cajamarca. Elevation is 1500 to 3000 m (5000 to 10,000 ft).

Puna — upper Andean slopes and plateaus in the highlands from Cajamarca southward; this includes the altiplano region between the two main Andean ranges. Elevation is 3400 to 4500+ m (11,000 to 15,000+ ft).

Humid Temperate — east slope of the Eastern Andes throughout the country; included is the páramo. Elevation is 2500 to 3400 m (8000 to 11,000 ft).

Humid Subtropical — east slope of the Eastern Andes throughout the country. Elevation is 1500 to 2500 m (5000 to 8000 ft).

Humid Upper Tropical — east slope of the Eastern Andes throughout the country; also upper slopes and crests of outlying mountains. Elevation is 900 to 1500 m (3000 to 5000 ft).

Humid Tropical — all terrain east of the Andes; includes lowlands, foothills, and lower slopes of the main Andes. Elevation is 150 to 900 m (500 to 3000 ft).

Habitats

We have divided Peru into 23 habitat types. Much of the descriptive information on habitats is drawn from the excellent works by Tosi (1960), and the Oficina Nacional de Evaluación de Recursos Naturales (1976). These are listed, described, and numbered below. Habitat numbers are assigned in the far right-hand column on the list of species. A maximum of three habitats is assigned; where a species occurs in more than three, the symbol '+' is used.

1. **Humid *terra firme* forest.** This is the mature, generally tall forest found on high ground in the lowlands, foothills, and on the lower slopes of the Andes. Here one finds the most diverse vegetation in the world; specific tree genera are too numerous to mention. For characteristics of this and the next category see *The Tropical Rain Forest: An Ecological Study* (Richards 1966). (Figure 1)

2. **Humid low-lying forest.** Herein is included seasonally inundated forest and permanently swampy forest; usually this habitat type borders rivers. Most flooding occurs during and just after the rainy season of November to May. Though this habitat is not considered mature in terms of tree species composition, some trees as tall as 60 m can be found. Fig trees (*Ficus*) are conspicuous in the seasonally

Figure 1. Humid Tropical Zone. Undergrowth of humid *terra firme* forest. Río Santiago, 180 m (590 ft), Dpto. Amazonas. September 1979. J. P. O'Neill.

Figure 2. Humid Tropical Zone. Humid low-lying forest, seasonally inundated. Río Heath, 185 m (600 ft), Dpto. Madre de Dios. June 1977. J. P. O'Neill.

flooded forest, while *Mauritia* palms are characteristic of the swamps. Extensive stands of these palms are known as *aguajales*. Seasonally flooded forest along the banks of the larger tributaries of the Amazon has been termed *varzea*. (Figures 2 and 3)

3. Forest edge, second growth. This habitat is primarily man-created. Included here are all types of early secondary growth, from grass-shrub associations to secondary forest. The latter is characterized by such fast-growing trees as *Cecropia* spp. Some bird species that were probably once restricted to river edge growth (described below in category 5) are now widespread in these second-growth situations. In the forested highlands, early successional stages appear where landslides have occurred. (Figure 4)

Figure 3. Humid Tropical Zone. *Heliconia* thicket in seasonally-inundated humid low-lying forest. Río Santiago, 180 m (590 ft), Dpto. Amazonas. September 1979. J. P. O'Neill.

Figure 4. Humid Upper Tropical Zone. Humid forest edge. East of La Peca, 900 m (3000 ft), Dpto. Amazonas. August 1978. M. D. Williams.

4. Tropical savanna, scrub. Various palms, especially *Mauritia*, shrubs, and grasses typify this habitat, which in Peru is mainly restricted to a small area along the Río Heath in the extreme southeastern portion of the country (see Graham *et al.* 1980). Other isolated areas of savanna scrub occur in San Martín. (Figures 5 and 6)

Figure 5. Humid Tropical Zone. *Mauritia* palm savanna. Pampa de Heath, 185 m (600 ft), Dpto. Madre de Dios. June 1977. J. P. O'Neill.

Figure 6. Humid Tropical Zone. Isolated woodland in tropical savanna. Pampa de Heath, 200 m (640 ft), Dpto. Madre de Dios. June 1977. J. P. O'Neill.

5. Tropical rivers and their margins. Rivers and their sandy or muddy shores attract relatively few birds, but many species inhabit the thickets of shrubs and trees (such as *Salix* and *Tessaria*) that quickly become established on the newly formed sand banks. Even more birds frequent the trees such as *Cecropia*, *Ficus*, and *Erythrina* that replace the early thicket species in a later successional stage. Dense stands of tall cane (*Gynerium*) are also typical of this habitat type, which has been termed *zabolo*. (Figures 7 and 8)

Figure 7. Humid Tropical Zone. River edge sand bank and recent growth (left) and seasonally flooded forest (right). Río Heath, 185 m (600 ft), Dpto. Madre de Dios. June 1977. J. P. O'Neill.

Figure 8. Humid Tropical Zone. River edge growth, mainly *Cecropia* and *Gynerium* cane. Río Heath, 185 m (600 ft), Dpto. Madre de Dios. June 1977. J. P. O'Neill.

17

6. Oxbow lakes and their margins. Most of the marsh vegetation in lowland eastern Peru borders oxbow lakes, which are former sections of rivers, now isolated as a result of the meandering nature of their parent streams. Along the edges of these oxbows are floating mats of grasses (*e.g. Paspalum*) and other aquatic plants like *Eichhornia*, *Pistia*, and the magnificent lily pads of *Victoria amazonica*. Such marshes are eventually invaded by shrubs and then trees; the latter vegetational stage is included in this category, along with the fringe of tall forest bordering the lake shore. (Figure 9)

Figure 9. Humid Tropical Zone. Marsh vegetation at end of oxbow lake. Yarinococha, 170 m (550 ft), Dpto. Ucayali. J. P. O'Neill.

Figure 10. Humid Upper Tropical Zone. Humid montane forest. Cordillera Colán, east of La Peca, 1200 m (4000 ft), Dpto. Amazonas. August 1978. M. D. Williams.

18

7. Humid montane forest. This habitat type comprises mature forest on mountain slopes and valleys, mainly on Amazon-facing slopes. Trees are characteristically laden with epiphytes such as bromeliads, orchids, ferns and mosses. Tree ferns (*Cyathea* and *Alsophila*) and bamboo (especially *Chusquea*) are conspicuous components. Though many tree genera are represented, at upper elevations *Clusia*, *Ocotea*, *Podocarpus*, *Weinmannia* and various members of the Melastomataceae are especially prominent. (Figure 10)

8. Elfin forest. This is the stunted forest that occurs at or near the crests of ridges and at treeline. As in the humid montane forest, arboreal epiphytes are abundant. Conspicuous tree genera include *Clusia*, *Gynoxys*, *Podocarpus*, and *Polylepis*. (Figures 11 and 12)

Figure 11. Humid Temperate Zone. Grazed páramo grassland and elfin forest groves. Mashua, on Tayabamba-Ongon trail, 3500 m (11,500 ft), Dpto. La Libertad. September 1979. J. W. Eley.

Figure 12. Humid Temperate Zone. Elfin forest interior. Unchog, Carpish Mountains, 2900 m (9500 ft), Dpto. Huánuco. July 1975. T. A. Parker III.

19

9. *Páramo* (or *jalca*). This is the humid grass-shrub association that borders the upper limits of Temperate Zone forest along the entire length of the Eastern Andes and also the Western Andes from Piura to Cajamarca. In areas free from burning and grazing, grasses (*Calamagrostris, Festuca*) can be quite tall. In disturbed places and near the forest edge shrubs are common, including *Brachyotum, Gynoxys, Hesperomeles, Hypericum* and *Senecio*. Terrestrial bromeliads (*Puya*) and ferns (*Lomaria*) are also conspicuous elements of this habitat. Small lakes dot the grasslands and bogs occur in poorly-drained areas. (Figure 13)

10. *Puna.* This includes the expansive, dry grasslands of the altiplano. Dominant grasses are *Calamagrostris, Festuca* and *Stipa*. In some areas bushes and shrubs are common, especially of the genera *Astragalus, Baccharis, Berberis, Ephedra, Lepidophyllum, Lupinus* and *Senecio*. (Figures 14 and 15)

Figure 13. Humid Temperate Zone. Undisturbed parámo grass-shrubland, with prominent terrestrial bromeliads and ferns. Cordillera Colán, east of La Peca, 3200 m (10,500 ft), Dpto. Amazonas. 25 August 1978. M. D. Williams.

Figure 14. Puna Zone. Puna grassland and saline lake. Laguna Salinas, east of Arequipa, 4300 m (14,000 ft), Dpto. Arequipa. June 1974. T. A. Parker III.

11. Montane lakes, streams, and their margins; marshes. Three types of lake are included here. These are (1) shallow to deep glacial pools with relatively little edge vegetation; (2) usually shallow, often large lakes with a fringe of relatively tall marsh growth (*e.g. Typha* and *Scirpus*); and (3) saline lakes, which are shallow and often contain water only seasonally.

12. Montane scrub. This is a broad category that includes a variety of plant associations, all characterized by shrubs, cacti, and short, scattered trees. Typical plant genera include those listed for the puna, other shrubs such as *Franseria* and *Lycium*, and the easily recognized cactus genera *Cereus* and *Opuntia*. Also present, especially in ravines and along streams, are trees such as *Acacia*, *Alnus*, *Caesalpinia*, *Jacaranda*, and *Schinus*. Several species of *Agave* are also common, as are terrestrial bromeliads (especially *Puya*). (Figure 16)

Figure 15. Puna Zone. Puna grassland. Along railway between Juliaca and Cuzco, Dpto. Puno, 4000 m (13,000 ft). December 1978. M. D. Williams.

Figure 16. Arid Subtropical Zone. Montane scrub. Cordillera Negra, west slope, 2000 m (6500 ft), Dpto. Ancash. June 1975. T. A. Parker III.

13. *Polylepis* woodlands. This is an important habitat for Andean birds. Groves and thickets of *Polylepis* (Rosaceae) trees and shrubs occur on steep, rocky slopes. They are usually isolated from other forest types and are often surrounded by puna grassland. These groves occur within an elevational range of 3400 to 4300 m (11,000 to 14,000 ft), but because of their structure and avian inhabitants they are considered part of the Arid Temperate Zone. The shrubs *Gynoxys*, *Brachyotum*, *Chuquiraga* and *Vernonia* are often associated with this habitat, as are the trees *Buddleia* and *Escallonia*. Epiphytic mistletoes (*Tristerix* and *Ligaria*) provide flowers and fruit for a variety of hummingbirds and several cotingas. (Figures 17 and 18)

Figure 17. Arid Temperate Zone. *Polylepis* woodland from a distance. Upper Santa Eulalia Valley, 3500 m (11,500 ft). Dpto. Lima. May 1978. T. A. Parker III.

Figure 18. Arid Temperate Zone. *Polylepis* woodland. Quebrada Tutapac, south of Yanac, 4300 m (14,000 ft), Dpto. Ancash. May 1976. T. A. Parker III.

14. Desert scrub. This is an association of generally scattered, short trees, shrubs and cacti. The trees and shrubs *Capparis*, *Cordia*, *Acacia* and *Prosopis* are characteristic of northwestern Peru and the dry Marañón River valley. In many areas columnar cacti (*Cereus*) are very conspicuous. (Figure 19)

Figure 19. Arid Tropical Zone. Desert scrub, mainly *Capparis* trees and shrubs. 4 km north of Ñaupe, Dpto. Lambayeque. May 1978. M. D. Williams.

15. Dry forest. These deciduous forests occur mainly on the lower slopes of the Western Andes from Tumbes to Cajamarca and also on the slopes of the dry regions of the Marañón, Éne, Apurimac, and Urubamba River valleys. Among the conspicuous tree genera are *Bombax*, *Bursera*, *Erythrina*, *Loxopterygium*, *Tabebuia* and various *Bombacaceae*. Epiphytic *Tillandsia* are common. (Figures 20 and 21)

16. Riparian thickets in tropical and subtropical deserts. In the north, extensive groves (called *algarrobales*) of *Prosopis* border rivers and streams, most of which are dry except for a few months of the year. Willows (*Salix*) grow along the banks of more permanent streams. Farther south *Salix*, *Schinus*, and *Tessaria* are the main components of this habitat.

17. Agricultural areas. Important here is the cover provided by trees and shrubbery growing along the edges of fields and around habitations. *Alnus*, *Eucalyptus* and *Salix* are common in these situations in the highlands.

Figure 20. Arid Tropical Zone. Dry deciduous forest. Extreme northwest of Peru, Campo Verde, 800 m (2500 ft), Dpto. Tumbes. June 1979. T. S. Schulenberg.

Figure 21. Arid Tropical Zone. Deciduous forest with *Bombax* trees in foreground. 15 km west of Canchaque, 500m (1500 ft), Dpto. Piura. June 1978. T.A. Parker III.

24

18. Mangroves. Swamps of mangroves occur along the shore of Tumbes. A few wide-ranging bird species are found only in this habitat within Peru.

19. Sandy, rocky deserts. The barren deserts of coastal Peru from Piura to Tacna are a northern extension of the Atacama Desert. These rocky or sandy deserts are interrupted by numerous river valleys and irrigated agricultural lands. Great expanses of the Atacama Desert are almost entirely devoid of vegetation, although terrestrial *Tillandsia* can grow even in the most barren areas. (Figures 22 and 23)

20. Coastal marshes. Marshes are scattered along the entire coastline; most are brackish and occur within a few hundred yards of the shore. Most conspicuous among various marsh plants are *Typha* and *Scirpus*. See Hughes (1970) for more on the plants and birds of this habitat.

Figure 22. Arid Subtropical Zone. Barren desert. North of Lima along Panamerican Highway, sea level, Dpto. Lima. T. A. Parker III.

Figure 23. Arid Subtropical Zone. Terrestrial *Tillandsia* bromeliads in coastal desert. South of Puerto Viejo, sea level, Dpto. Lima. J. P. O'Neill.

25

21. Coastal beaches, mudflats. Sandy shores characterize much of northern Peru, while rocky and sandy beaches alternate from central Peru south to the Chilean border. Along stretches of the coastline impressive cliffs rise above the water. These provide nesting and resting sites for many seabirds, as do the *guano* islands offshore (see Murphy 1925).

22. Coastal waters. The waters of the Humboldt Current are well known for their seabirds, especially for the *guano*-producing cor-

Figure 24. Sea and Shore. Peruvian Boobies (*Sula variegata*) on Isla Lobos de Tierra, Dpto. Lambayeque. July 1978. M.D. Williams.

Figure 25. Sea and Shore. Islas Ballestas, southwest of Pisco, Dpto. Ica. December 1978. M. D. Williams.

morants and boobies. This cold north-flowing current moves out into the Pacific at the latitude of Talara in Peru, and warm-water seabirds are found from there northward. All waters within three miles of the shore are considered coastal. Pelagic species such as albatrosses, shearwaters and petrels are generally found more frequently beyond this rather arbitrary limit. (Figures 24, 25, 26, and 27)

23. Pelagic waters. These are waters beyond three miles offshore.

Figure 26. Sea and Shore. Peruvian Pelicans (*Pelecanus thagus*) on Islas Ballestas, southwest of Pisco, Dpto. Ica. December 1978. M. D. Williams.

Figure 27. Sea and Shore. Inshore waters. Pisco, Dpto. Ica. August 1975. M. A. Plenge.

27

THE CHECKLIST

	sea and shore	arid tropical	arid subtropical	arid temperate	humid subtropical and temperate	puna	humid temperate	humid subtropical	humid upper tropical	humid tropical	habitats

PENGUINS — Spheniscidae

	sea and shore	arid tropical	arid subtropical	arid temperate	humid subtropical and temperate	puna	humid temperate	humid subtropical	humid upper tropical	humid tropical	habitats
Humboldt Penguin — *Spheniscus humboldti*	U										22

RHEAS — Rheidae

	sea and shore	arid tropical	arid subtropical	arid temperate	humid subtropical and temperate	puna	humid temperate	humid subtropical	humid upper tropical	humid tropical	habitats
Lesser Rhea — *Pterocnemia pennata*											
Puna Rhea — *P. tarapacensis*						sR					10

TINAMOUS — Tinamidae

	sea and shore	arid tropical	arid subtropical	arid temperate	humid subtropical and temperate	puna	humid temperate	humid subtropical	humid upper tropical	humid tropical	habitats
Gray Tinamou — *Tinamus tao*									U	U	1,7
Black Tinamou — *T. osgoodi*									sR	sR	1,7
Great Tinamou — *T. major*										F	1,2
White-throated Tinamou — *T. guttatus*										U	1,2
Highland Tinamou — *Nothocercus bonapartei*							nR				7
Tawny-breasted Tinamou — *N. julius*							R				7,8
Hooded Tinamou — *N. nigrocapillus*								U			7
Cinereous Tinamou — *Crypturellus cinereus*										U	2
Little Tinamou — *C. soui*										F	1,2
Brown Tinamou — *C. obsoletus*							F	F		R	1,7
Undulated Tinamou — *C. undulatus*										F	2,3,5
Rusty Tinamou — *C. brevirostris*										?	?
Bartlett's Tinamou — *C. bartletti*										F	1,2
Variegated Tinamou — *C. variegatus*										U	1
Red-legged Tinamou — *C. atrocapillus*										F	2,3
Pale-browed Tinamou — *C. transfasciatus*		nF									15
Brazilian Tinamou — *C. strigulosus*										?	?
Small-billed Tinamou — *C. parvirostris*										sR	3,5
Tataupa Tinamou — *C. tataupa*		cR									16
Red-winged Tinamou — *Rhynchotus rufescens*										sF	4
Taczanowski's Tinamou — *Nothoprocta taczanowskii*			R								12
Kalinowski's Tinamou — *N. kalinowskii*			U								12
Ornate Tinamou — *N. ornata*						U					10
Andean Tinamou — *N. pentlandii*			U	F							12,13
Curve-billed Tinamou — *N. curvirostris*							U				9,17
Darwin's Nothura — *Nothura darwinii*						U					10
Puna Tinamou — *Tinamotis pentlandii*						U					10

GREBES — Podicipedidae

	sea and shore	arid tropical	arid subtropical	arid temperate	humid subtropical and temperate	puna	humid temperate	humid subtropical	humid upper tropical	humid tropical	habitats
Least Grebe — *Podiceps dominicus*		R								R	6,20
White-tufted Grebe — *P. [Rollandia] rolland*	C					C					11,20
Puna Grebe — *P. taczanowskii*						cU					11
Silvery Grebe — *P. occipitalis*						F					11
Great Grebe — *P. major*	/F										22

	WEST						EAST				
	sea and shore	arid tropical	arid subtropical	arid temperate	humid subtropical and temperate	puna	humid temperate	humid subtropical	humid upper tropical	humid tropical	habitats
Short-winged Grebe — *Centropelma [Rollandia] micropterum*						sF					11
Pied-billed Grebe — *Podilymbus podiceps*	U									?	20
ALBATROSSES — Diomedeidae											
*Royal Albatross — *Diomedea epomophora*	mR										23
Galapagos Albatross — *D. irrorata*	mU										23
Black-browed Albatross — *D. melanophrys*	mF										23
Buller's Albatross — *D. bulleri*	mR										23
White-capped Albatross — *D. cauta*	mR										23
*Gray-headed Albatross — *D. chrysostoma*	mR										23
SHEARWATERS — Procellariidae											
Giant Fulmar — *Macronectes giganteus*	mF										22,23
Southern Fulmar — *Fulmarus glacialoides*	mU										22,23
Cape Petrel — *Daption capense*	mF										22,23
Dark-rumped Petrel — *Pterodroma phaeopygia*	m?										23
Blue-footed Petrel — *P. cookii*	m?										23
Broad-billed Prion — *Pachyptila vittata*	mR										?
Medium-billed Prion — *P. salvini*	mR										?
Dove Prion — *P. desolata*	mR										22
Slender-billed Prion — *P. belcheri*	mU										22
Gray Petrel — *Adamastor [Procellaria] cinereus*	mR										23
White-chinned Petrel (or Shoemaker) — *Procellaria aequinoctialis*	mU										22,23
Parkinson's Petrel — *P. parkinsoni*	m?										23
Pink-footed Shearwater — *Puffinus creatopus*	mF										23
Buller's (New Zealand) Shearwater — *P. bulleri*	m?										23
Sooty Shearwater — *P. griseus*	mC										22,23
*Little Shearwater — *P. assimilis*	mR										23
STORM-PETRELS — Hydrobatidae											
Wilson's Storm-Petrel — *Oceanites oceanicus*	mC										22,23
White-vented Storm-Petrel — *O. gracilis*	C										22,23
White-faced Storm-Petrel — *Pelagodroma marina*	m?										23
Black-bellied Storm-Petrel — *Fregetta tropica*	m?										23
*Least Storm-Petrel — *Halocyptena microsoma*	m?										23
Wedge-rumped Storm-Petrel — *Oceanodroma tethys*	U										23
Sooty Storm-Petrel — *O. markhami*	U										22,23
Black Storm-Petrel — *O. melania*	m?										23
Ringed Storm-Petrel — *O. hornbyi*	U										23

	WEST						EAST				
	sea and shore	arid tropical	arid subtropical	arid temperate	humid subtropical and temperate	puna	humid temperate	humid subtropical	humid upper tropical	humid tropical	habitats
DIVING-PETRELS — Pelecanoididae											
Peruvian Diving-Petrel — *Pelecanoides garnotii*	F										22
TROPICBIRDS — Phaethontidae											
Red-billed Tropicbird — *Phaethon aethereus*	R										23
PELICANS — Pelecanidae											
Brown Pelican — *Pelecanus occidentalis*	nF										22
Peruvian Pelican — *P. thagus*	C										22
BOOBIES — Sulidae											
Blue-footed Booby — *Sula nebouxii*	nC										22
Peruvian Booby — *S. variegata*	C										22
Masked Booby — *S. dactylatra*	R										23
CORMORANTS — Phalacrocoracidae											
Neotropic Cormorant — *Phalacrocorax olivaceus*	C	F				U				F	5,6,22
Guanay Cormorant — *P. bougainvillii*	C										22
Red-legged Cormorant — *P. gaimardi*	C										22
DARTERS — Anhingidae											
American Darter (or Anhinga) — *Anhinga anhinga*						R				U	6
FRIGATEBIRDS — Fregatidae											
Magnificent Frigatebird — *Fregata magnificens*	nC										22
HERONS — Ardeidae											
White-necked Heron — *Ardea cocoi*	R	R				R				F	5,6,20
Great Egret — *Egretta alba*	F	U				?				F	5,6,20
Snowy Egret — *E. thula*	C	U				U				F	6,20,21
Little Blue Heron — *Hydranassa caerulea*	U									R	20
Louisiana Heron — *H. tricolor*	R										20
Striated Heron — *Butorides striatus*	U	U								U	6,20
Chestnut-bellied Heron — *Agamia agami*										R	2,6
Cattle Egret — *Ardeola ibis*	C	C				U				U	17
Capped Heron — *Pilherodius pileatus*										F	5,6
Black-crowned Night-Heron — *Nycticorax nycticorax*	U					F				R	5,6,11
Yellow-crowned Night-Heron — *N. violacea*	nF										18
Rufescent Tiger-Heron — *Tigrisoma lineatum*										U	2,6
Fasciated Tiger-Heron — *T. fasciatum*							U	U	U		11
Zigzag Heron — *Zebrilus undulatus*										R	2
*Stripe-backed Bittern — *Ixobrychus involucris*										mR	6
Least Bittern — *I. exilis*	R	R								R	6,20

31

	WEST						EAST				
	sea and shore	arid tropical	arid subtropical	arid temperate	humid subtropical and temperate	puna	humid temperate	humid subtropical	humid upper tropical	humid tropical	habitats
BOAT-BILLED HERONS — Cochleariidae											
(Southern) Boat-billed Heron — *Cochlearius cochlearius*										R	6
STORKS — Ciconiidae											
Wood Stork — *Mycteria americana*	nR					R				U	5
Jabiru — *Jabiru mycteria*	R					R				R	5
IBISES — Threskiornithidae											
Black-faced Ibis — *Theristicus melanopis*	R	R	R			U					11,17
Green Ibis — *Mesembrinibis cayennensis*										U	2,6
White Ibis — *Eudocimus albus*	nF										18
*White-faced Ibis — *Plegadis chihi*	sR										20
Puna Ibis — *P. ridgwayi*	R					C					11
Roseate Spoonbill — *Ajaia ajaja*	nR									R	5,18
FLAMINGOS — Phoenicopteridae											
Greater Flamingo — *Phoenicopterus ruber* †Chilean Flamingo — *P. chilensis*	lC					lC					11,21
Andean Flamingo — *Phoenicoparrus andinus*						lU					11
Puna (James') Flamingo — *P. jamesi*						lF					11
SCREAMERS — Anhimidae											
Horned Screamer — *Anhima cornuta*										F	5,6
*Southern Screamer — *Chauna torquata*										R	5
DUCKS AND GEESE — Anatidae											
Fulvous Whistling-Duck — *Dendrocygna bicolor*	R					R				R	5,17,20
White-faced Whistling-Duck — *D. viduata*	R					R				R	5,20
Black-bellied Whistling-Duck — *D. autumnalis*	R									R	5,20
Andean Goose — *Chloephaga melanoptera*						C					11
Orinoco Goose — *Neochen jubata*										R	5
Crested Duck — *Lophonetta specularioides*						F	U				11
Speckled Teal — *Anas flavirostris*				F		C	U				11
White-cheeked Pintail — *A. bahamensis*	C										20,22
Yellow-billed Pintail — *A. georgica*	U					C					11,20
Silver Teal — *A. versicolor* †Puna Teal — *A. puna*	R					C					11
Blue-winged Teal — *A. discors*	mR	mU				m?				m?	20
Cinnamon Teal — *A. cyanoptera*	C					C					11,20
Red Shoveler — *A. platalea*						sR					11
Torrent Duck — *Merganetta armata*				U	U	R	U	U			11
Southern Pochard — *Netta erythrophthalma*	R	R				R					11,20

	WEST							EAST			
	sea and shore	arid tropical	arid subtropical	arid temperate	humid subtropical and temperate	puna	humid temperate	humid subtropical	humid upper tropical	humid tropical	habitats
Comb Duck — *Sarkidiornis melanotos* / American Comb Duck — *S. sylvicola*	R	R	R								17,20
Muscovy Duck — *Cairina moschata*		R								U	5,6
Ruddy Duck — *Oxyura jamaicensis* / Andean Duck — *O. ferruginea*	U					F	U				11,20
Masked Duck — *O. dominica*		R	R							R	6,20
AMERICAN VULTURES — Cathartidae											
Andean Condor — *Vultur gryphus*	U	U	U	U	U	U	U				+
King Vulture — *Sarcoramphus papa*		U							U	U	+
Black Vulture — *Coragyps atratus*		C	C							F	+
Turkey Vulture — *Cathartes aura*	C	C	C	U	U	R	U	U	U	F	+
Lesser Yellow-headed Vulture — *C. burrovianus*										/R	4,5,6
Greater Yellow-headed Vulture — *C. melambrotus*										F	1,2
HAWKS AND EAGLES — Accipitridae											
Pearl Kite — *Gampsonyx swainsonii*		U								U	3,17
Swallow-tailed Kite — *Elanoides forficatus*		nU						U	U	U	1,2,3
Gray-headed Kite — *Leptodon cayanensis*										U	2
Hook-billed Kite — *Chondrohierax uncinatus*		?	R		?		R	U	U	U	1,7
Double-toothed Kite — *Harpagus bidentatus*										U	1,2
Plumbeous Kite — *Ictinia plumbea*										C	3
Snail Kite — *Rostrhamus sociabilis*										R	6
Slender-billed Kite — *Helicolestes [Rostrhamus] hamatus*										U	6
Bicolored Hawk — *Accipiter bicolor*		R								R	1,2
Tiny Hawk — *A. superciliosus*										R	1,2
Semicollared Hawk — *A. collaris*								R			7
Gray-bellied Hawk — *A. poliogaster*										R	?
Sharp-shinned Hawk — *A. striatus* / †Plain-breasted Hawk — *A. ventralis*					U		U	U			7
Black-chested Buzzard-Eagle — *Geranoaetus melanoleucus*		U	U	U	?		U				12
*White-tailed Hawk — *Buteo albicaudatus*										sU	4
Red-backed Hawk — *B. polyosoma*		F	U	F	F		U	U	R		+
Puna (or Variable) Hawk — *B. poecilochrous*						F					10
Zone-tailed Hawk — *B. albonotatus*		R	R							R	3
Swainson's Hawk — *B. swainsoni*		mR								mR	3,17
Broad-winged Hawk — *B. platypterus*			mR							mU	1
Roadside Hawk — *B. magnirostris*		?						F	F	F	3,5

33

| | WEST | | | | | | EAST | | | | |
	sea and shore	arid tropical	arid subtropical	arid temperate	humid subtropical and temperate	puna	humid temperate	humid subtropical	humid upper tropical	humid tropical	habitats
White-rumped Hawk — *B. leucorrhous*					R		R	R			7
White-throated Hawk — *B. albigula*					R		U	U			7
Short-tailed Hawk — *B. brachyurus*										F	3
Gray Hawk — *B. nitidus*										R	2,5
Bay-winged Hawk — *Parabuteo unicinctus*		U	R								14,16
White Hawk — *Leucopternis albicollis*									U	U	1,7
*Gray-backed Hawk — *L. occidentalis*		nU									15
Black-faced Hawk — *L. melanops*										R	1
White-browed Hawk — *L. kuhli*										R	1,2
Slate-colored Hawk — *L. schistacea*										U	2
Plumbeous Hawk — *L. plumbea*		n?									?
Black-collared Hawk — *Busarellus nigricollis*										U	5,6
Savanna Hawk — *Heterospizias meridionalis*		F								/U	4,17
Common Black Hawk — *Buteogallus anthracinus* †Mangrove Black Hawk — *B. subtilis*		nF									18
Great Black Hawk — *B. urubitinga*		U								F	5,15
Solitary Eagle — *Harpyhaliaetus solitarius*					R		R	R		?	7
Crested Eagle — *Morphnus guianensis*										R	1,2
Harpy Eagle — *Harpia harpyja*										R	1,2
Black-and-Chestnut Eagle — *Oroaetus isidori*							R	R			7
Black-and-White Hawk-Eagle — *Spizastur melanoleucus*										R	3,5,6
Ornate Hawk-Eagle — *Spizaetus ornatus*										U	1
Black Hawk-Eagle — *S. tyrannus*		nR								U	1
Cinereous Harrier — *Circus cinereus*	R	R				F					11,20
Crane Hawk — *Geranospiza caerulescens*		nU								R	2,15
OSPREYS — Pandionidae Osprey — *Pandion haliaetus*	mF									mU	5,6,21
FALCONS — Falconidae Laughing Falcon — *Herpetotheres cachinnans*		R								U	2,5,6
Collared Forest-Falcon — *Micrastur semitorquatus*		nR								R	1,2
Buckley's Forest-Falcon — *M. buckleyi*										?	?
Slaty-backed Forest-Falcon — *M. mirandollei*										U	1,2
Barred Forest-Falcon — *M. ruficollis*									U	U	1,2,7
†Lined Forest-Falcon — *M. gilvicollis*										R	2
Black Caracara — *Daptrius ater*										F	3,5,6
Red-throated Caracara — *D. americanus*									U	U	1,2,7

34

| | WEST | | | | | | | EAST | | | |
Species	sea and shore	arid tropical	arid subtropical	arid temperate	humid subtropical and temperate	puna	humid temperate	humid subtropical	humid upper tropical	humid tropical	habitats
Yellow-headed Caracara — *Milvago chimachima*										lC	3,5,6
Mountain Caracara — *Phalcoboenus megalopterus*					U	C	U				9,10,12
Crested Caracara — *Polyborus plancus*		F	sR							sU	4,14,17
Peregrine Falcon — *Falco peregrinus*	mR	mR	mR	?	?	mR	?	?	?	mR	+
Orange-breasted Falcon — *F. deiroleucus*										R	3,5
Bat Falcon — *F. rufigularis*		R						R	R	F	3,5,6
Aplomado Falcon — *F. femoralis*		U	U	U	U	F	U			lU	+
Merlin — *F. columbarius*		m?									?
American Kestrel — *F. sparverius*		U	F	F		C	U	R			+

CHACHALACAS, GUANS, AND CURASSOWS — Cracidae

Species	sea and shore	arid tropical	arid subtropical	arid temperate	humid subtropical and temperate	puna	humid temperate	humid subtropical	humid upper tropical	humid tropical	habitats
Rufous-headed Chachalaca — *Ortalis erythroptera*		nU									15
Variable Chachalaca — *O. motmot* †Speckled Chachalaca — *O. guttata*										F	2,3,5
Bearded Guan — *Penelope barbata*					U		nU				7
Andean Guan — *P. montagnii*						F	F				7
Spix's Guan — *P. jacquacu*										F	1,2
White-winged Guan — *P. albipennis*		R									15
Common (Blue-throated) Piping-Guan — *Aburria [Pipile] pipile*										U	1,2,5
Wattled Guan — *A. aburri*								U	U		7
Sickle-winged Guan — *Chamaepetes goudotii*							sR	U	U		7
Nocturnal Curassow — *Nothocrax urumutum*										R	1,2
Salvin's Curassow — *Crax [Mitu] salvini*										nU	1
Razor-billed Curassow — *C. [Mitu] mitu*										R	1
Southern Helmeted Curassow — *C. [Pauxi] unicornis*									R		7
Wattled Curassow — *C. globulosa*										R	?

PARTRIDGES AND QUAIL — Phasianidae

Species	sea and shore	arid tropical	arid subtropical	arid temperate	humid subtropical and temperate	puna	humid temperate	humid subtropical	humid upper tropical	humid tropical	habitats
Marbled Wood-Quail — *Odontophorus gujanensis*										U	1
Rufous-breasted Wood-Quail — *O. speciosus*								U	U	?	1,7
Stripe-faced Wood-Quail — *O. balliviani*								sU			7
Starred Wood-Quail — *O. stellatus*										F	1

HOATZINS — Opisthocomidae

Species	sea and shore	arid tropical	arid subtropical	arid temperate	humid subtropical and temperate	puna	humid temperate	humid subtropical	humid upper tropical	humid tropical	habitats
Hoatzin — *Opisthocomus hoazin*										C	5,6

	WEST							EAST			
	sea and shore	arid tropical	arid subtropical	arid temperate	humid subtropical and temperate	puna	humid temperate	humid subtropical	humid upper tropical	humid tropical	habitats
LIMPKINS — Aramidae											
Limpkin — *Aramus guarauna*										R	6
TRUMPETERS — Psophiidae											
Gray-winged Trumpeter — *Psophia crepitans*										nR	1
Pale-winged Trumpeter — *P. leucoptera*										R	1,2
RAILS — Rallidae											
Plumbeous Rail — *Rallus [Ortygonax] sanguinolentus*	C	R	U			C					11,20
Blackish Rail — *R. [Ortygonax] nigricans*										R	6
Clapper Rail — *R. longirostris*	nF										18
Lesser (or Virginia) Rail — *R. limicola*	U										20
Peruvian Rail — *R. peruvianus*				?		?					?
Spotted Rail — *R. [Pardirallus] maculatus*		R									6
Uniform Crake — *Amaurolimnas concolor*										R	6
Gray-necked Wood-Rail — *Aramides cajanea*										F	2,5,6
Red-winged Wood-Rail — *A. calopterus*										U	1,2
Chestnut-headed Crake — *Anurolimnas castaneiceps*										U	1,2,3
Sora Crake — *Porzana carolina*										mR	6
Ash-throated Crake — *P. albicollis*										sU	4
Black Crake — *Laterallus jamaicensis*	R										20
Gray-breasted Crake — *L. exilis*										R	6
Rufous-sided Crake — *L. melanophaius*										F	6
Black-banded Crake — *L. fasciatus*										R	3,6
Russet-crowned Crake — *L. viridis*										R	3,6
Ocellated Crake — *Micropygia schomburgkii*										sR	4
Paint-billed Crake — *Neocrex erythrops*	R	R	R								20
Spot-flanked Gallinule — *Porphyriops melanops*										?	?
Common Gallinule — *Gallinula chloropus*	C					C					6,11,20
Purple Gallinule — *Porphyrula martinica*										R	6
Azure Gallinule — *P. flavirostris*										sU	6
American Coot — *Fulica americana*	U					C					11,20
†Slate-colored Coot — *F. ardesiaca*	R					F					11,20
Red-fronted Coot — *F. rufifrons*	sR										20
Giant Coot — *F. gigantea*						lC					11
FINFOOTS OR SUNGREBES — Heliornithidae											
American Finfoot (or Sungrebe) — *Heliornis fulica*										U	6

	sea and shore	arid tropical	arid subtropical	arid temperate	humid subtropical and temperate	puna	humid temperate	humid subtropical	humid upper tropical	humid tropical	habitats
SUNBITTERNS — Eurypygidae											
Sunbittern — *Eurypyga helias*							R	U		U	2,5,6
JACANAS — Jacanidae											
Wattled Jacana — *Jacana jacana*		nR								U	6
OYSTERCATCHERS — Haematopodidae											
Common Oystercatcher — *Haematopus ostralegus*											
†American Oystercatcher — *H. palliatus*	F										21
Blackish Oystercatcher — *H. ater*	F										21
PLOVERS — Charadriidae											
Andean Lapwing — *Vanellus resplendens*	R					C	U				9,11
Pied Lapwing — *Hoploxypterus [Vanellus] cayanus*										F	5
Black-bellied Plover — *Pluvialis squatarola*	mC									mR	21
American Golden Plover — *P. dominica*	mR					mR				mU	5,20
Semipalmated Plover — *Charadrius semipalmatus*	mC										21
Snowy Plover — *C. alexandrinus*	F										21
Puna Plover — *C. alticola*	mU					lF					11,20,21
Collared Plover — *C. collaris*	nU	U								F	5
Killdeer — *C. vociferus*	C		C								17,20
Wilson's Plover — *C. wilsonia*	nU										21
Rufous-chested Dotterel — *Zonibyx [Charadrius] modestus*	mR										21
Tawny-throated Dotterel — *Oreopholus [Eudromias] ruficollis*		U	U			U					10,17,19
Diademed Sandpiper-Plover — *Phegornis mitchellii*						R					11
SANDPIPERS AND SNIPES — Scolopacidae											
Surfbird — *Aphriza virgata*	mF										21
Ruddy Turnstone — *Arenaria interpres*	mC										21
Solitary Sandpiper — *Tringa solitaria*	mR	mR								mR	5,6,20
Lesser Yellowlegs — *T. flavipes*	mC					mC				mU	5,11,20
Greater Yellowlegs — *T. melanoleuca*	mC					mF				mU	5,21
Spotted Sandpiper — *Actitis macularia*	mF	mU	mU			mR				mF	5,6,20
Wandering Tattler — *Heteroscelus incanus*	mU					mR					21
Willet — *Catoptrophorus semipalmatus*	mF										21
Red Knot — *Calidris canutus*	mF										21
Least Sandpiper — *C. minutilla*	mC					?					20,21
Baird's Sandpiper — *C. bairdii*	mU					mC					11,20,21

	WEST						EAST				
	sea and shore	arid tropical	arid subtropical	arid temperate	humid subtropical and temperate	puna	humid temperate	humid subtropical	humid upper tropical	humid tropical	habitats
White-rumped Sandpiper — *C. fuscicollis*	mR					?				mU	5,20,21
Pectoral Sandpiper — *C. melanotos*	mC					mF				mF	5,20
Semipalmated Sandpiper — *C. pusilla*	mC										21
Western Sandpiper — *C. mauri*	mC										21
Sanderling — *C. alba*	mC					mR				mR	21
*Dunlin — *C. alpina*	mR										21
Curlew Sandpiper — *C. ferruginea*	mR										21
Stilt Sandpiper — *Micropalama himantopus*	mF					mU				mU	5,20,21
Buff-breasted Sandpiper — *Tryngites subruficollis*	mR									mU	3,5
*Ruff — *Philomachus pugnax*	mR										20
Upland Sandpiper — *Bartramia longicauda*	mR					mR	mU	mU		mF	3
Whimbrel — *Numenius phaeopus*	mF					mR					21
Hudsonian Godwit — *Limosa haemastica*	mR										20,21
Marbled Godwit — *L. fedoa*	mR										21
Long-billed Dowitcher — *Limnodromus scolopaceus*	m?										21
Short-billed Dowitcher — *L. griseus*	mC										21
Common Snipe — *Gallinago gallinago* / South American Snipe — *G. paraguaiae*										R	5
†Puna Snipe — *G. andina*						F	U				11
Cordilleran Snipe — *G. stricklandii* / Andean Snipe — *G. jamesoni*					R		F				9
Banded Snipe — *G. imperialis*							R				8

STILTS AND AVOCETS — Recurvirostridae

	sea and shore	arid tropical	arid subtropical	arid temperate	humid subtropical and temperate	puna	humid temperate	humid subtropical	humid upper tropical	humid tropical	habitats
Black-necked Stilt — *Himantopus mexicanus*	C					F					11,20
Andean Avocet — *Recurvirostra andina*						sF					11

PHALAROPES — Phalaropodidae

	sea and shore	arid tropical	arid subtropical	arid temperate	humid subtropical and temperate	puna	humid temperate	humid subtropical	humid upper tropical	humid tropical	habitats
Red Phalarope — *Phalaropus fulicarius*	mC										22,23
Northern Phalarope — *P. [Lobipes] lobatus*	mU										22,23
Wilson's Phalarope — *P. [Steganopus] tricolor*	mC					mC				mU	20

THICK-KNEES — Burhinidae

	sea and shore	arid tropical	arid subtropical	arid temperate	humid subtropical and temperate	puna	humid temperate	humid subtropical	humid upper tropical	humid tropical	habitats
Peruvian Thick-knee — *Burhinus superciliaris*	lF	lF	lF								14,17,19

SEEDSNIPES — Thinocoridae

	sea and shore	arid tropical	arid subtropical	arid temperate	humid subtropical and temperate	puna	humid temperate	humid subtropical	humid upper tropical	humid tropical	habitats
Rufous-bellied Seedsnipe — *Attagis gayi*						lC					10
Gray-breasted Seedsnipe — *Thinocorus orbignyianus*						C					10
Least Seedsnipe — *T. rumicivorus*	lC	lC	lC								19

	sea and shore	arid tropical	arid subtropical	arid temperate	humid subtropical and temperate	puna	humid temperate	humid subtropical	humid upper tropical	humid tropical	habitats
SKUAS AND JAEGERS — Stercoriidae											
Great Skua — *Catharacta skua*											
Chilean Skua — *C. chilensis*	mF										22,23
South Polar Skua — *C. maccormicki*	m?										?
Pomarine Jaeger — *Stercorarius pomarinus*	mU										22,23
Parasitic Jaeger — *S. parasiticus*	mU										22,23
Long-tailed Jaeger — *S. longicaudus*	mR										23
GULLS AND TERNS — Laridae											
Gray Gull — *Larus modestus*	mC										21,22
Band-tailed Gull — *L. belcheri*	mC										21,22
Kelp Gull — *L. dominicanus*	mC										21,22
Laughing Gull — *L. atricilla*	nF										21,22
Gray-hooded Gull — *L. cirrocephalus*	F										20,21
Andean Gull — *L. serranus*	mU		U			C	U				11,21
Franklin's Gull — *L. pipixcan*	mC				mR					mR	17,21,22
Sabine's Gull — *Xema sabini*	mU										22,23
Swallow-tailed Gull — *Creagrus furcatus*	mF										22,23
Black Tern — *Chlidonias niger*	mR										20,22
Large-billed Tern — *Phaetusa simplex*										F	5,6
Gull-billed Tern — *Gelochelidon nilotica*	mR										20,21
South American Tern — *Sterna hirundinacea*	F										21,22
Common Tern — *S. hirundo*	mC										21,22
Arctic Tern — *S. paradisaea*	mC										22,23
*Snowy-crowned (Trudeau's) Tern — *S. trudeaui*	mR										21
*Sooty Tern — *S. fuscata*	mR										23
Yellow-billed Tern — *S. superciliaris*										F	5,6
*Least Tern — *S. albifrons*	mR										21
Peruvian Tern — *S. lorata*	C										21,22
Royal Tern — *S. [Thalasseus] maxima*	mF										21,22
Elegant Tern — *S. [Thalasseus] elegans*	mC										21,22
Sandwich Tern — *S. [Thalasseus] sandvicensis*	mU										21,22
Inca Tern — *Larosterna inca*	C										22
SKIMMERS — Rynchopidae											
Black Skimmer — *Rynchops niger*	lC					R				F	5,21,22
PIGEONS AND DOVES — Columbidae											
Rock Dove — *Columba livia*			iC								+
Band-tailed Pigeon — *C. fasciata*					F		F	F			7
Scaled Pigeon — *C. speciosa*									U	U	4,5,7
Spot-winged Pigeon — *C. maculosa*			sU								12,13

	sea and shore	arid tropical	arid subtropical	arid temperate	humid subtropical and temperate	puna	humid temperate	humid subtropical	humid upper tropical	humid tropical	habitats
Pale-vented Pigeon — *C. cayennensis*										C	3,5,6
Peruvian Pigeon — *C. oenops*			cF								15
Ruddy Pigeon — *C. subvinacea*									U	U	1,2
Plumbeous Pigeon — *C. plumbea*		nR						U	C	C	1,2,7
Eared Dove — *Zenaida auriculata*		F	C	C	U	U	R				+
White-winged Dove — *Z. asiatica*		C	C								16,17
Plain-breasted Ground-Dove — *Columbina minuta*			/U								17
Ruddy Ground-Dove — *C. talpacoti*										C	3,5
Ecuadorean Ground-Dove — *C. buckleyi*		nU									3,15
Picui Ground-Dove — *C. picui*										sF	3,5
Croaking Ground-Dove — *C. cruziana*		C	C								+
Blue Ground-Dove — *Claravis pretiosa*		cF								F	3,5
Maroon-chested Ground-Dove — *C. mondetoura*					R			R			7
Bare-faced Ground-Dove — *Metriopelia ceciliae*			F	F							12
Golden-spotted Ground-Dove — *M. aymara*					sF						10,17
Black-winged Ground-Dove — *M. melanoptera*				F							12,13
Ochre-bellied Dove — *Leptotila ochraceiventris*		n?									15
White-tipped Dove — *L. verreauxi*		F	F					F	?	U	3,16
Gray-fronted Dove — *L. rufaxilla*										F	2,3,5
Sapphire Quail-Dove — *Geotrygon saphirina*									nU		7
Ruddy Quail-Dove — *G. montana*										F	1,2
White-throated Quail-Dove — *G. frenata*				U			U	U	U		7
PARROTS — Psittacidae											
Blue-and-Yellow Macaw — *Ara ararauna*										U	+
Military Macaw — *A. militaris*					R				/U		7
Scarlet Macaw — *A. macao*										U	1,2
Red-and-Green Macaw — *A. chloroptera*										U	1
Chestnut-fronted Macaw — *A. severa*										F	2
Red-bellied Macaw — *A. manilata*										/C	2,4
Blue-headed Macaw — *A. couloni*										/F	1
Red-shouldered Macaw — *A. nobilis*										sF	4
Scarlet-fronted Parakeet — *Aratinga wagleri*		cC	cC	U	U		U				7,15,17
Mitred Parakeet — *A. mitrata*							/C				7,17
Red-masked Parakeet — *A. erythrogenys*		C									15,16
White-eyed Parakeet — *A. leucophthalmus*										C	+
Dusky-headed Parakeet — *A. weddellii*										C	2,5,6
Peach-fronted Parakeet — *A. aurea*										sF	4

| | WEST | | | | | | | EAST | | | |
	sea and shore	arid tropical	arid subtropical	arid temperate	humid subtropical and temperate	puna	humid temperate	humid subtropical	humid upper tropical	humid tropical	habitats
Golden-plumed Parakeet — *Leptosittaca branickii*							/U				7,8
Painted Parakeet — *Pyrrhura picta*									/F	/F	1,7
Maroon-tailed Parakeet — *P. melanura*									nU	nU	1,7
†Berlepsch's Parakeet — *P. berlepschi*									nU	nU	1,7
Rock Parakeet — *P. rupicola*										sF	1,2
Mountain Parakeet — *Bolborhynchus aurifrons*			/F	/F	/C		U				12,16,17
Barred Parakeet — *B. lineola*							U				7
Andean Parakeet — *B. orbygnesius*			/C			?	?				12
Blue-winged Parrotlet — *Forpus xanthopterygius*										F	3,5
Dusky-billed Parrotlet — *F. sclateri*										U	1,2
Pacific Parrotlet — *F. coelestis*		C									14,15,16
Yellow-faced Parrotlet — *F. xanthops*		cC									14,15,16
Canary-winged Parakeet — *Brotogeris versicolurus*			iU							C	2,3,5
Gray-cheeked Parakeet — *B. pyrrhopterus*		nF									15
Cobalt-winged Parakeet — *B. cyanoptera*										C	+
Tui Parakeet — *B. sanctithomae*										nC	2,5,6
*Sapphire-rumped Parrotlet — *Touit purpurata*										n?	2
Scarlet-shouldered Parrotlet — *T. huetii*										/U	1,2
Spot-winged Parrotlet — *T. stictoptera*								nR			7
Black-headed Parrot — *Pionites melanocephala*										nF	1,2
White-bellied Parrot — *P. leucogaster*										F	1,2
Orange-cheeked Parrot — *Pionopsitta barrabandi*										F	1,2
Black-eared Parrot — *Hapalopsittaca melanotis*							R				7,8
*Rusty-faced Parrot — *H. amazonina*							nR				7
Short-tailed Parrot — *Graydidascalus brachyurus*										/C	2,5,6
Blue-headed Parrot — *Pionus menstruus*									F	C	+
Red-billed Parrot — *P. sordidus*								F	C		3,7
Plum-crowned Parrot — *P. tumultuosus*							U				7
†White-capped Parrot — *P. seniloides*							nU				7
Bronze-winged Parrot — *P. chalcopterus*		nU									15
Festive Parrot — *Amazona festiva*										nF	2
Yellow-headed Parrot — *A. ochrocephala*										F	1,2
Orange-winged Parrot — *A. amazonica*										U	2,5
Scaly-naped Parrot — *A. mercenaria*							F	F	?		7
Mealy Parrot — *A. farinosa*										F	1,2
Red-fan Parrot — *Deroptyus accipitrinus*										n?	?

	sea and shore	arid tropical	arid subtropical	arid temperate	humid subtropical and temperate	puna	humid temperate	humid subtropical	humid upper tropical	humid tropical	habitats
CUCKOOS AND ANIS — Cuculidae											
*Ash-colored Cuckoo — *Coccyzus cinereus*										sR	2
Black-billed Cuckoo — *C. erythropthalmus*		mR								mR	?
Yellow-billed Cuckoo — *C. americanus*										mU	2,3
Dark-billed Cuckoo — *C. melacoryphus*		cU	R							U	3,5,15
Gray-capped Cuckoo — *C. lansbergi*			mR								?
Squirrel Cuckoo — *Piaya cayana*		nF								C	+
Black-bellied Cuckoo — *P. melanogaster*										U	1,2
Little Cuckoo — *P. minuta*										U	5,6
Greater Ani — *Crotophaga major*										lC	2,5
Smooth-billed Ani — *C. ani*									U	C	3,5,6
Groove-billed Ani — *C. sulcirostris*		C	C								16,17
Striped Cuckoo — *Tapera naevia*		nU								F	3,4
Pheasant Cuckoo — *Dromococcyx phasianellus*										R	1,2
Pavonine Cuckoo — *D. pavoninus*									?	R	1,2
Rufous-vented Ground-Cuckoo — *Neomorphus geoffroyi*										R	1,2
Red-billed Ground-Cuckoo — *N. pucheranii*										R	1,2
BARN OWLS — Tytonidae											
Barn Owl — *Tyto alba*		U	U	U							17
TYPICAL OWLS — Strigidae											
Vermiculated Screech-Owl — *Otus guatemalae*										?	1
West Peruvian Screech-Owl — *O. roboratus*		U	U	U							13,15
Otus — sp. nov.		U									16
Tropical Screech-Owl — *O. choliba*										F	3,5
Rufescent Screech-Owl — *O. ingens*							U	U			7
Otus — sp. nov.							nU				7
Tawny-bellied Screech-Owl — *O. watsonii*										F	1,2
Cloud-forest Screech-Owl — *O. marshalli*							s?				7
White-throated Screech-Owl — *O. albogularis*					F		U	U			7
Crested Owl — *Lophostrix cristata*										U	1,2
Great Horned Owl — *Bubo virginianus*			U	U	R						12
Spectacled Owl — *Pulsatrix perspicillata*		R								F	1,2,15
Band--bellied Owl — *P. melanota*									F	F	1,7
Least Pygmy-Owl — *Glaucidium minutissimum*										lF	1,2
Andean Pygmy-Owl — *G. jardinii*					U		F	U	R		7,8
Ferruginous Pygmy-Owl — *G. brasilianum*		C	F							F	+
Long-whiskered Owlet — *Xenoglaux loweryi*							nR	nR			8
Burrowing Owl — *Athene [Speotyto] cunicularia*		F	F	F		F					+

	sea and shore	arid tropical	arid subtropical	arid temperate	humid subtropical and temperate	puna	humid temperate	humid subtropical	humid upper tropical	humid tropical	habitats
WEST								**EAST**			
Black-and-White Owl — *Ciccaba nigrolineata*		n?									?
Black-banded Owl — *C. huhula*									R	R	1,2
Mottled Owl — *C. virgata*										R	1,2
Rufous-banded Owl — *C. albitarsus*					F		F	F			7
Striped Owl — *Rhinoptynx clamator*		R								/U	3,4
Short-eared Owl — *Asio flammeus*	R					U					10,20
Buff-fronted Owl — *Aegolius harrisii*					R		R				7
OILBIRDS — Steatornithidae											
Oilbird — *Steatornis caripensis*							R	U	U	/C	1,7
POTOOS — Nyctibiidae											
Great Potoo — *Nyctibius grandis*										U	2,5,6
Long-tailed Potoo — *N. aethereus*										?	?
Common Potoo — *N. griseus*		R							U	F	3,5,6
White-winged Potoo — *N. leucopterus*									nR		7
Rufous Potoo — *N. bracteatus*										R	2
NIGHTHAWKS — Caprimulgidae											
*Semicollared Nighthawk — *Lurocalis semitorquatus*										R	1,2,3
Rufous-bellied Nighthawk — *L. rufiventris*							U	U			3,7
Sand-colored Nighthawk — *Chordeiles rupestris*										/C	5
Lesser Nighthawk — *C. acutipennis*		F	U							?	14,16,17
Common Nighthawk — *C. minor*		mR								m?	+
*Band-tailed Nighthawk — *Nyctiprogne leucopyga*										n?	5
Nacunda Nighthawk — *Podager nacunda*										R	3,4,5
Pauraque — *Nyctidromus albicollis*		U		U						F	3,5
Ocellated Poorwill — *Nyctiphrynus ocellatus*									U	U	1,2
*Rufous Nightjar — *Caprimulgus rufus*										?	?
Silky-tailed Nightjar — *C. sericocaudatus*										R	3
Band-winged Nightjar — *C. longirostris*		R	F	F			U	U			3,12,13
Spot-tailed Nightjar — *C. maculicaudus*										/F	3,4
Little Nightjar — *C. parvulus*										R	3
Scrub Nightjar — *C. anthonyi*		U									14,15
Blackish Nightjar — *C. nigrescens*										/F	3,4
Ladder-tailed Nightjar — *Hydropsalis climacocerca*										/F	5,6
Scissor-tailed Nightjar — *H. brasiliana*										?	5
Swallow-tailed Nightjar — *Uropsalis segmentata*							U				3,8,9
Lyre-tailed Nightjar — *U. lyra*									U	U	3,7

	sea and shore	arid tropical	arid subtropical	arid temperate	humid subtropical and temperate	puna	humid temperate	humid subtropical	humid upper tropical	humid tropical	habitats
SWIFTS — Apodidae											
White-collared Swift — *Streptoprocne zonaris*		R	R	U	U		lC	lC	lC	lC	+
Chestnut-collared Swift — *Cypseloides rutilus*				U	U		F	F			7,12
White-chinned Swift — *C. cryptus*									?	?	?
Chapman's Swift — *Chaetura chapmani*										R	3,5
Chimney Swift — *C. pelagica*			lC	R						?	+
Gray-rumped Swift — *C. cinereiventris*		nF							lC	U	3,5,7
Pale-rumped Swift — *C. egregia*										R	3,5
Short-tailed Swift — *C. brachyura*		lF								lC	1,2,3
White-tipped Swift — *Aeronautes montivagus*					lC		lC	lC			3,7
Andean Swift — *A. andecolus*			lC	lC							12
Lesser Swallow-tailed Swift — *Panyptila cayennensis*		nR								U	3
Fork-tailed Palm-Swift — *Reinarda [Tachornis] squamata*										C	2,5,6
HUMMINGBIRDS — Trochilidae											
Blue-fronted Lancebill — *Doryfera johannae*									U	?	7
Green-fronted Lancebill — *D. ludoviciae*								U	U		7
Rufous-breasted Hermit — *Glaucis hirsuta*										C	2,5,6
Pale-tailed Barbthroat — *Threnetes leucurus*									U	U	1,2
Green Hermit — *Phaethornis guy*								U	F		7
Tawny-bellied Hermit — *P. syrmatophorus*								nC			7
Long-tailed Hermit — *P. superciliosus*		nF								F	1,2
White-bearded Hermit — *P. hispidus*										F	2,5
Straight-billed Hermit — *P. bourcieri*										nU	1
Koepcke's Hermit — *P. koepckeae*									U	?	1
Needle-billed Hermit — *P. philippi*										U	1
Reddish Hermit — *P. ruber*										lC	1,2
White-browed Hermit — *P. stuarti*										sU	1,2
Gray-chinned Hermit — *P. griseogularis*		R			U						7,15
Little Hermit — *P. longuemareus*										lF	3
White-tipped Sicklebill — *Eutoxeres aquila*									nU	nU	1,7
Buff-tailed Sicklebill — *E. condamini*								U	U		7
Gray-breasted Sabrewing — *Campylopterus largipennis*										U	2,3,5
Swallow-tailed Hummingbird — *Eupetomena macroura*									lF	lU	3,4
White-necked Jacobin — *Florisuga mellivora*										U	1,2
Brown Violetear — *Colibri delphinae*									R		7
Green Violetear — *C. thalassinus* †Mountain Violetear — *C. cyanotus*							R	C	F		3

44

	sea and shore	arid tropical	arid subtropical	arid temperate	humid subtropical and temperate	puna	humid temperate	humid subtropical	humid upper tropical	humid tropical	habitats
Sparkling Violetear — *C. coruscans*		R	U	C	F		U	U	R	R	+
Green-breasted Mango — *Anthracothorax prevostii*		nU									15
Black-throated Mango — *A. nigricollis*										F	3,5
Violet-headed Hummingbird — *Klais guimeti*									U		7
Rufous-crested Coquette — *Lophornis delattrei*										U	1,2
Spangled Coquette — *L. stictolopha*										?	?
Festive Coquette — *L. chalybea*										R	1,2
Wire-crested Thorntail — *Popelairia popelairii*									R	/U	1
Black-bellied Thorntail — *P. langsdorffi*										R	?
Blue-chinned Sapphire — *Chlorestes notatus*										/F	3
Blue-tailed Emerald — *Chlorostilbon mellisugus*								R	U	F	1,2,7
Fork-tailed Woodnymph — *Thalurania furcata*									U	F	1,2
Violet-bellied Hummingbird — *Damophila julie*					nF						3
Rufous-throated Sapphire — *Hylocharis sapphirina*										?	?
White-chinned Sapphire — *H. cyanus*										U	2
Golden-tailed Sapphire — *Chrysuronia oenone*										U	2,3
White-tailed Goldenthroat — *Polytmus guainumbi*										sF	4
Green-tailed Goldenthroat — *P. theresiae*										/F	4
Tumbes Hummingbird — *Leucippus baeri*		nF									14,15
Spot-throated Hummingbird — *L. taczanowskii*		cF									14,15
Olive-spotted Hummingbird — *L. chlorocercus*										R	3
Many-spotted Hummingbird — *Taphrospilus hypostictus*									?	?	3?
Green-and-White Hummingbird — *Amazilia viridicauda*								sF	?		3
White-bellied Hummingbird — *A. chionogaster*							F	F	F	U	3
Glittering-throated Emerald — *A. fimbriata*										U	3,5
Sapphire-spangled Emerald — *A. lactea*										F	3,5
Andean Emerald — *A. franciae*			cF								12
Amazilia Hummingbird — *A. amazilia*		C	C								14,15,16
White-vented Plumeleteer — *Chalybura buffonii*					nU						7
Speckled Hummingbird — *Adelomyia melanogenys*					U			F	F		7
Whitetip — *Urosticte benjamini*								nU			7
Ecuadorean Piedtail — *Phlogophilus hemileucurus*									/F		7
Peruvian Piedtail — *P. harterti*									R		7
Gould's Jewelfront — *Polyplancta aurescens*										U	1,2
Fawn-breasted Brilliant — *Heliodoxa rubinoides*								U			7

	WEST						EAST				
	sea and shore	arid tropical	arid subtropical	arid temperate	humid subtropical and temperate	puna	humid temperate	humid subtropical	humid upper tropical	humid tropical	habitats
Violet-fronted Brilliant — *H. leadbeateri*								U	F		7
Black-throated Brilliant — *H. schreibersii*									nU	nR	1,7
Pink-throated Brilliant — *H. gularis*									nR		7
Rufous-webbed Brilliant — *H. branickii*									sU		7
Fiery Topaz — *Topaza pyra*										nR	1,2
Andean Hillstar — *Oreotrochilus estella*				F	F						12,13
Black-breasted Hillstar — *O. melanogaster*				cU	cU						12,13
White-tailed Hillstar — *Urochroa bougueri*									nR		7
Giant Hummingbird — *Patagona gigas*				F							12,13
Shining Sunbeam — *Aglaeactis cupripennis*				lC			U				8,12,13
White-tufted Sunbeam — *A. castelnaudii*				lC			lR				8,12
Purple-backed Sunbeam — *A. aliciae*				cR							12
Mountain Velvetbreast — *Lafresnaya lafresnayi*					U		U				3,7
Great Sapphirewing — *Pterophanes cyanopterus*							F				8,9
Bronzy Inca — *Coeligena coeligena*								F			7
Collared Inca — *C. torquata*							C				7
Buff-winged Starfrontlet — *C. lutetiae*							nC				7,8,9
Violet-throated Starfrontlet — *C. violifer*							C				7,8,9
Rainbow Starfrontlet — *C. iris*					nC						7
Sword-billed Hummingbird — *Ensifera ensifera*					R		U				7,8
Chestnut-breasted Coronet — *Boissonneaua matthewsii*							F				7
Amethyst-throated Sunangel — *Heliangelus amethysticollis*							C				7
Tourmaline Sunangel — *H. exortis*							nF				7
Purple-throated Sunangel — *H. viola*					nC						7
Royal Sunangel — *H. regalis*								nC			3,7
Glowing Puffleg — *Eriocnemis vestitus*							nC				3,9
Sapphire-vented Puffleg — *E. luciani*							U				7,8
Emerald-bellied Puffleg — *E. alinae*								U			7
Greenish Puffleg — *Haplophaedia aureliae*								U	U		7
Booted Rackettail — *Ocreatus underwoodii*								U	U		7
Black-tailed Trainbearer — *Lesbia victoriae*				lF			U				3,12
Green-tailed Trainbearer — *L. nuna*				F			R				3,12
Red-tailed Comet — *Sappho sparganura*							s?	s?			12
Bronze-tailed Comet — *Polyonymus caroli*				U							12
Purple-backed Thornbill — *Ramphomicron microrhynchum*							R				7,8
Black Metaltail — *Metallura phoebe*				C							12
Neblina Metaltail — *M. odomae*							nF				9

| | WEST | | | | | | EAST | | | | |
	sea and shore	arid tropical	arid subtropical	arid temperate	humid subtropical and temperate	puna	humid temperate	humid subtropical	humid upper tropical	humid tropical	habitats
Coppery Metaltail — *M. theresiae*							cC				9
Scaled Metaltail — *M. aeneocauda*							sF				9
Fire-throated Metaltail — *M. eupogon*							cF				9
Tyrian Metaltail — *M. tyrianthina*				lU	C		F				7,8,9
Rufous-capped Thornbill — *Chalcostigma ruficeps*							U	U			3,7
Olivaceous Thornbill — *C. olivaceum*				U		U					10,12
Blue-mantled Thornbill — *C. stanleyi*							sF				9,13
Rainbow-bearded Thornbill — *C. herrani*							nF				9
Bearded Mountaineer — *Oreonympha nobilis*				sU							12
Mountain Avocetbill — *Opisthoprora euryptera*							lU				7
Gray-bellied Comet — *Tephrolesbia griseiventris*				cR							12
Long-tailed Sylph — *Aglaiocercus kingi*								F			7
Wedge-billed Hummingbird — *Schistes geoffroyi*								U	U		7
Black-eared Fairy — *Heliothryx aurita*									U	U	1,2,7
Marvelous Spatuletail — *Loddigesia mirabilis*							nU	nU			3,12
Long-billed Starthroat — *Heliomaster longirostris*	U									U	3,15
Oasis Hummingbird — *Rhodopis vesper*			U								12,16
Peruvian Sheartail — *Thaumastura cora*	U	F									12,16
Amethyst Woodstar — *Calliphlox amethystina*										U	1,2,3
Purple-collared Woodstar — *Myrtis fanny*			F	F							12
*Chilean Woodstar — *Eulidia yarrellii*		sR									16
Short-tailed Woodstar — *Myrmia micrura*	U										14
White-bellied Woodstar — *Acestrura mulsant*							lF	U			3,7
Little Woodstar — *A. bombus*							?	?	?		?
TROGONS — Trogonidae											
Crested Quetzal — *Pharomachrus antisianus*							U	U			7
Golden-headed Quetzal — *P. auriceps*				nU			F	U			7
Pavonine Quetzal — *P. pavoninus*									lR	lU	1,2
Black-tailed Trogon — *Trogon melanurus*		R								F	2,5,6
White-tailed Trogon — *T. viridis*										C	1,2
Collared Trogon — *T. collaris*										F	1,2
Masked Trogon — *T. personatus*							F	F	U		7
Black-throated Trogon — *T. rufus*										R	?
Blue-crowned Trogon — *T. curucui*									lF	lF	2,3
Violaceous Trogon — *T. violaceus*		nR								F	1,2

		WEST							EAST		
	sea and shore	arid tropical	arid subtropical	arid temperate	humid subtropical and temperate	puna	humid temperate	humid subtropical	humid upper tropical	humid tropical	habitats
KINGFISHERS — Alcedinidae											
Ringed Kingfisher — *Ceryle torquata*		R								F	5,6
Amazon Kingfisher — *Chloroceryle amazona*										F	5,6
Green Kingfisher — *C. americana*		R	R						U	F	5,6
Green-and-Rufous Kingfisher — *C. inda*										U	2,6
Pygmy Kingfisher — *C. aenea*										U	2,6
MOTMOTS — Momotidae											
Broad-billed Motmot — *Electron platyrhynchum*										F	1,2
Rufous Motmot — *Baryphthengus ruficapillus*										F	1,2
Blue-crowned Motmot — *Momotus momota*		nF								F	1,2
Highland Motmot — *M. aequatorialis*								U			7
JACAMARS — Galbulidae											
Chestnut Jacamar — *Galbalcyrhynchus leucotis*										lF	2,6
Purus Jacamar — *G. purusianus*										?	?
Brown Jacamar — *Brachygalba lugubris*										nU	3
White-throated Jacamar — *B. albogularis*										sR	3,5
Yellow-billed Jacamar — *Galbula albirostris*										nF	1
Blue-cheeked Jacamar — *G. cyanicollis*										lF	1,2
White-chinned Jacamar — *G. tombacea*										n?	2
Bluish-fronted Jacamar — *G. cyanescens*									R	F	1,2,3
Bronzy Jacamar — *G. leucogastra*										nR	?
Paradise Jacamar — *G. dea*										R	2
Great Jacamar — *Jacamerops aurea*										U	2
PUFFBIRDS — Bucconidae											
White-necked Puffbird — *Notharchus macrorhynchus*										U	1,2
Pied Puffbird — *N. tectus*										R	3
Chestnut-capped Puffbird — *Bucco macrodactylus*										U	2,3
Spotted Puffbird — *B. tamatia*										nU	2
Collared Puffbird — *B. capensis*										R	1
White-eared Puffbird — *Nystalus chacuru*			cU							lU	4,15
Striolated Puffbird — *N. striolatus*										F	1,2
White-chested Puffbird — *Malacoptila fusca*										nU	1,2
Semicollared Puffbird — *M. semicincta*										sU	1,2
Black-streaked Puffbird — *M. fulvogularis*								U			7
Rufous-necked Puffbird — *M. rufa*										n?	?
Lanceolated Monklet — *Micromonacha lanceolata*									R		7

	sea and shore	arid tropical	arid subtropical	arid temperate	humid subtropical and temperate	puna	humid temperate	humid subtropical	humid upper tropical	humid tropical	habitats
								WEST		EAST	
Rusty-breasted Nunlet — *Nonnula rubecula*										nR	?
Fulvous-chinned Nunlet — *N. sclateri*										cR	2
Brown Nunlet — *N. brunnea*										n?	1
Gray-cheeked Nunlet — *N. ruficapilla*									R	R	2,3
White-faced Nunbird — *Hapaloptila castanea*							nR				7
Black-fronted Nunbird — *Monasa nigrifrons*										C	1,2,3
White-fronted Nunbird — *M. morphoeus*										C	1,2
Yellow-billed Nunbird — *M. flavirostris*										R	2,3
Swallow-winged Puffbird — *Chelidoptera tenebrosa*										F	3,5
BARBETS — Capitonidae											
Scarlet-crowned Barbet — *Capito aurovirens*										F	2
Black-spotted Barbet — *C. niger*										C	1,2
Lemon-throated Barbet — *Eubucco richardsoni*										U	1,2
Red-headed Barbet — *E. bourcierii*									nU		7
Scarlet-hooded Barbet — *E. tucinkae*									sR	sR	1,2,7
Versicolored Barbet — *E. versicolor*								U	U		7
TOUCANS — Ramphastidae											
Chestnut-tipped Toucanet — *Aulacorhynchus derbianus*									U		7
Emerald Toucanet — *A. prasinus*								F	U	R	1,2,7
Blue-banded Toucanet — *A. coeruleicinctus*								sU			7
Yellow-browed Toucanet — *A. huallagae*								cU			7
Chestnut-eared Aracari — *Pteroglossus castanotis*										C	2,3
Many-banded Aracari — *P. pluricinctus*										nF	1,2
Lettered Aracari — *P. inscriptus*										F	2,3
Ivory-billed Aracari — *P. flavirostris*										F	1,2
†Brown-mandibled Aracari — *P. mariae*										F	1,2
Curl-crested Aracari — *P. beauharnaesii*										lU	1,2
Golden-collared Toucanet — *Selenidera reinwardtii*									U	F	1,2
Gray-breasted Mountain-Toucan — *Andigena hypoglauca*							U				7
Hooded Mountain-Toucan — *A. cucullata*							sU				7
Yellow-ridged Toucan — *Ramphastos culminatus*									sR	F	1,2
Black-mandibled Toucan — *R. ambiguus*									U		7
Cuvier's Toucan — *R. cuvieri*										C	1,2
*Toco Toucan — *R. toco*										sR	4

49

WOODPECKERS — Picidae

	WEST							EAST			
	sea and shore	arid tropical	arid subtropical	arid temperate	humid subtropical and temperate	puna	humid temperate	humid subtropical	humid upper tropical	humid tropical	habitats
Rufous-breasted Piculet — *Picumnus rufiventris*										U	2,3,5
Plain-breasted Piculet — *P. castelnau*										/U	3,5
Marcapata Piculet — *P. subtilis*										s?	?
Bar-breasted Piculet — *P. borbae*										sU	1,2
Gold-fronted Piculet — *P. aurifrons*										F	1
Ocellated Piculet — *P. dorbygnianus*								U	U		7
Ecuadorean Piculet — *P. sclateri*		U									15
Speckle-chested Piculet — *P. steindachneri*								nU	nU		7
Andean Flicker — *Colaptes rupicola*			F	U	C	U					9,10,12
Spot-breasted Woodpecker — *Chrysoptilus punctigula*										F	1,2
Black-necked Woodpecker — *C. atricollis*			U	cU							12
Crimson-mantled Woodpecker — *Piculus rivolii*				F			F	F	U		7
Golden-Olive Woodpecker — *P. rubiginosus*		F							F		7,15,16
Yellow-throated Woodpecker — *P. flavigula*										R	1,2
White-throated Woodpecker — *P. leucolaemus*										U	1,2
Golden-Green Woodpecker — *P. chrysochloros*										U	1,2
Chestnut Woodpecker — *Celeus elegans*										U	1
Scale-breasted Woodpecker — *C. grammicus*										U	1,2
Cream-colored Woodpecker — *C. flavus*										U	2
Rufous-headed Woodpecker — *C. spectabilis*										R	2,5
Ringed Woodpecker — *C. torquatus*										R	1
Lineated Woodpecker — *Dryocopus lineatus*		U							U	F	3,5,6
Yellow-tufted Woodpecker — *Melanerpes cruentatus*									U	C	2,3
*White Woodpecker — *Leuconerpes candidus*										sR	4
White-fronted Woodpecker — *Trichopicus cactorum*			s?								12?
Smoky-Brown Woodpecker — *Veniliornis fumigatus*			U	/F	F			U	F		7,13
Little Woodpecker — *V. passerinus*										F	3,5
Red-stained Woodpecker — *V. affinis*										U	1,2
Red-rumped Woodpecker — *V. kirkii*		nR									15
Scarlet-backed Woodpecker — *V. callonotus*		F									14,15,16
Yellow-vented Woodpecker — *V. dignus*								R			7
Bar-bellied Woodpecker — *V. nigriceps*							U				7,8
Crimson-crested Woodpecker — *Phloeoceastes melanoleucus*										F	3,5,6
Guayaquil Woodpecker — *P. gayaquilensis*		U									15
Red-necked Woodpecker — *P. rubricollis*										F	1,2
Powerful Woodpecker — *P. pollens*							R				7
Crimson-bellied Woodpecker — *P. haematogaster*								R	R		7

WOODCREEPERS — Dendrocolaptidae

	sea and shore	arid tropical	arid subtropical	arid temperate	humid subtropical and temperate	puna	humid temperate	humid subtropical	humid upper tropical	humid tropical	habitats
Tyrannine Woodcreeper — *Dendrocincla tyrannina*							R	R			7
Plain-Brown Woodcreeper — *D. fuliginosa*		nR								F	1,2
White-chinned Woodcreeper — *D. merula*										/F	1,2
Long-tailed Woodcreeper — *Deconychura longicauda*										U	1,2
Spot-throated Woodcreeper — *D. stictolaema*										?	?
Olivaceous Woodcreeper — *Sittasomus griseicapillus*		nF							F	F	1,2,7
Wedge-billed Woodcreeper — *Glyphorhynchus spirurus*									F	C	1,2,7
Long-billed Woodcreeper — *Nasica longirostris*										R	2,6
Cinnamon-throated Woodcreeper — *Dendrexetastes rufigula*										U	2
Bar-bellied Woodcreeper — *Hylexetastes stresemanni*										R	1,2
Strong-billed Woodcreeper — *Xiphocolaptes promeropirhynchus*		nR					R	R	R	R	1,2,7
Barred Woodcreeper — *Dendrocolaptes certhia*										U	1,2
Black-banded Woodcreeper — *D. picumnus*									U	U	1
Straight-billed Woodcreeper — *Xiphorhynchus picus*										F	2,5,6
Striped Woodcreeper — *X. obsoletus*										U	1,2
Ocellated Woodcreeper — *X. ocellatus*									sF	/F	1,2
Spix's Woodcreeper — *X. spixii*										F	1
Elegant Woodcreeper — *X. elegans*										?	?
Buff-throated Woodcreeper — *X. guttatus*										C	1,2
Olive-backed Woodcreeper — *X. triangularis*							U	F			7
Streak-headed Woodcreeper — *Lepidocolaptes souleyetti*		F									15,16
Spot-crowned Woodcreeper — *L. affinis*					nF		F	F			7
Lineated Woodcreeper — *L. albolineatus*										U	1
Greater Scythebill — *Campylorhamphus pucherani*							R				7
Red-billed Scythebill — *C. trochilirostris*		nU					R	R		/U	2
Brown-billed Scythebill — *C. pusillus*								nR			7

OVENBIRDS — Furnariidae

	sea and shore	arid tropical	arid subtropical	arid temperate	humid subtropical and temperate	puna	humid temperate	humid subtropical	humid upper tropical	humid tropical	habitats
Grayish Miner — *Geositta maritima*			/F								19
Coastal Miner — *G. peruviana*	C	C									19
Dark-winged Miner — *G. saxicolina*						/C					10
Puna Miner — *G. punensis*						sC					10,12
Common Miner — *G. cunicularia*						C					10

51

	WEST						EAST				
	sea and shore	arid tropical	arid subtropical	arid temperate	humid subtropical and temperate	puna	humid temperate	humid subtropical	humid upper tropical	humid tropical	habitats
Slender-billed Miner — *G. tenuirostris*					F	F					10,17
Thick-billed Miner — *G. crassirostris*			lU	lU							12
Scale-throated Earthcreeper — *Upucerthia dumetaria*				s?							12
White-throated Earthcreeper — *U. albigula*			sF	sF							12
Plain-breasted Earthcreeper — *U. jelskii*				F		F					10,12
Striated Earthcreeper — *U. serrana*				F							12
Straight-billed Earthcreeper — *U. ruficauda*				sF							12
Stout-billed Cinclodes — *Cinclodes [Upucerthia] excelsior*						s?					?
Bar-winged Cinclodes — *C. fuscus*				U	U	C	U				9,10,11
White-winged Cinclodes — *C. atacamensis*						F					11
White-bellied Cinclodes — *C. palliatus*						lR					10
Seaside Cinclodes — *C. nigrofumosus* †Surf Cinclodes — *C. taczanowskii*	F										21
Pale-legged Hornero — *Furnarius leucopus*		C								U	5,16
†Pale-billed Hornero — *F. torridus*										n?	5
Lesser Hornero — *F. minor*										n?	5
Wren-like Rushbird — *Phleocryptes melanops*	C		C			C					11,20
Andean Tit-Spinetail — *Leptasthenura andicola*				lU							12,13
Streaked Tit-Spinetail — *L. striata*			U								12
Rusty-crowned Tit-Spinetail — *L. pileata*				lF							12,13
†White-browed Tit-Spinetail — *L. xenothorax*							sF				13
Plain-mantled Tit-Spinetail — *L. aegithaloides*			sF								16
Tawny Tit-Spinetail — *L. yanacensis*				lU			sU				13
Azara's Spinetail — *Synallaxis azarae*							C	C			3
Elegant Spinetail — *S. elegantior*					nF						3
Coursen's Spinetail — *S. courseni*							sU				3,7
Dusky Spinetail — *S. moesta*										?	?
Cabanis' Spinetail — *S. cabanisi*									U	R	3,5,6
Cinereous-breasted Spinetail — *S. hypospodia*										sF	4
Pale-breasted Spinetail — *S. albescens*										sR	5,6
Slaty Spinetail — *S. brachyura*					nF						3
Dark-breasted Spinetail — *S. albigularis*										C	3,5
Plain-crowned Spinetail — *S. gujanensis*										F	3,5
Marañón Spinetail — *S. maranonica*			cF								16
White-bellied Spinetail — *S. propinqua*										?	?
Blackish-headed Spinetail — *S. tithys*			nF								15
Rufous Spinetail — *S. unirufa*							F				7
Ruddy Spinetail — *S. rutilans*										lU	1,2

	WEST							EAST			
	sea and shore	arid tropical	arid subtropical	arid temperate	humid subtropical and temperate	puna	humid temperate	humid subtropical	humid upper tropical	humid tropical	habitats
Chestnut-throated Spinetail — *S. cherriei*										/U	1
Necklaced Spinetail — *S. stictothorax*		C									14
Russet-bellied Spinetail — *S. zimmeri*			cU								12
White-browed Spinetail — *S. [Hellmayrea] gularis*							U				8
Yellow-throated Spinetail — *Certhiaxis cinnamomea*										nU	5,6
Red-and-White Spinetail — *C. mustelina*										F	6
Ash-browed Spinetail — *Cranioleuca curtata*								U	U		7
†Fork-tailed Spinetail — *C. furcata*								n?	n?		?
Rusty-backed Spinetail — *C. vulpina*										U	3
Line-cheeked Spinetail — *C. antisiensis*			/F	/F	F						7,12,13
Marcapata Spinetail — *C. marcapatae*							F				7,8
Light-crowned Spinetail — *C. albiceps*							s?				7,8
Creamy-crested Spinetail — *C. albicapilla*			/F								12,13
Speckled Spinetail — *C. gutturata*										U	1,2
Great Spinetail — *Siptornopsis hypochondriacus*			cU								12
White-chinned Thistletail — *Schizoeaca fuliginosa*							F				9
†Mouse-colored Thistletail — *S. griseomurina*							nF				9
†Eye-ringed Thistletail — *S. palpebralis*							c?				9
†Puna Thistletail — *S. helleri*							sF				7,8,9
Creamy-breasted Canastero — *Asthenes dorbignyi*			sF	sF							12
Cordilleran Canastero — *A. modesta*						C					10
Cactus Canastero — *A. cactorum*			U								12
Canyon Canastero — *A. pudibunda*				F							12,13
Rusty-fronted Canastero — *A. ottonis*				sF				sR			12
Streak-backed Canastero — *A. wyatti*						/F					10
Austral Canastero — *A. anthoides* / Puno Canastero — *A. punensis*						s?					10
Streak-throated Canastero — *A. humilis*						C					10
Many-striped Canastero — *A. flammulata*				/F	/F		F				9
†Junin Canastero — *A. virgata*					/U		U				9,10
†Scribble-tailed Canastero — *A. maculicauda*							sU				9
Line-fronted Canastero — *A. urubambensis*							U				8,9,13
Plain Softtail — *Thripophaga fusciceps*										R	2,5
Russet-mantled Softtail — *T. berlepschi*							cR				8
Rufous-fronted Thornbird — *Phacellodomus rufifrons*		cC									14
Streak-fronted Thornbird — *P. striaticeps*				s?							14

	WEST							EAST			
	sea and shore	arid tropical	arid subtropical	arid temperate	humid subtropical and temperate	puna	humid temperate	humid subtropical	humid upper tropical	humid tropical	habitats
Chestnut-backed Thornbird — *P. dorsalis*			cU								12
Spectacled Prickletail — *Siptornis striaticollis*								nU			7
Equatorial Graytail — *Xenerpestes singularis*									nU		7
Orange-fronted Plushcrown — *Metopothrix aurantiacus*										/F	2,3
Pearled Treerunner — *Margarornis squamiger*					F		C	F			7,8
Rusty-winged Barbtail — *Premnornis guttuligera*								U			7
Spotted Barbtail — *Premnoplex brunnescens*								U	U		7
Streaked Tuftedcheek — *Pseudocolaptes boissonneautii*					nC		C	C			7,8
Striped Woodhaunter — *Hyloctistes subulatus*										U	1,2
Chestnut-winged Hookbill — *Ancistrops strigilatus*										U	1,2
Buff-browed Foliage-gleaner — *Syndactyla rufosuperciliata*								U	U		3,7
Lineated Foliage-gleaner — *S. subalaris*								nU	U		3,7
Peruvian Recurvebill — *Simoxenops ucayalae*										sR	1,2
Montane Foliage-gleaner — *Anabacerthia striaticollis*							F	F			7
Rufous-rumped Foliage-gleaner — *Philydor erythrocercus*									U	F	1
Cinnamon-rumped Foliage-gleaner — *P. pyrrhodes*										U	1,2
Buff-fronted Foliage-gleaner — *P. rufus*									U	R	1,2
Chestnut-winged Foliage-gleaner — *P. erythropterus*										U	1,2
Rufous-tailed Foliage-gleaner — *P. ruficaudatus*										U	1
Olive-backed Foliage-gleaner — *Automolus infuscatus*										F	1,2
Crested Foliage-gleaner — *A. dorsalis*										U	1
Ruddy Foliage-gleaner — *A. rubiginosus*									U	U	1
Buff-throated Foliage-gleaner — *A. ochrolaemus*									U	C	1,2,7
Chestnut-crowned Foliage-gleaner — *A. rufipileatus*										F	2,3,5
Rufous-necked Foliage-gleaner — *A. ruficollis*					U						7
Brown-rumped Foliage-gleaner — *A. melanopezus*										R	2
Henna-hooded Foliage-gleaner — *Hylocryptus erythrocephalus*		U									15
Flammulated Treehunter — *Thripadectes flammulatus*							nR				7

54

| | WEST | | | | | | | | EAST | | |
	sea and shore	arid tropical	arid subtropical	arid temperate	humid subtropical and temperate	puna	humid temperate	humid subtropical	humid upper tropical	humid tropical	habitats
Striped Treehunter — *T. holostictus*								U			7
Black-billed Treehunter — *T. melanorhynchus*									U		7
Buff-throated Treehunter — *T. scrutator*							R				7
Rufous-tailed Xenops — *Xenops milleri*										/U	1,2
Slender-billed Xenops — *X. tenuirostris*										R	1
Streaked Xenops — *X. rutilans*		nU			nU			U	F	R	1,7,15
Plain Xenops — *X. minutus*										F	1,2
Gray-throated Leafscraper — *Sclerurus albigularis*									R		7
Tawny-throated Leafscraper — *S. mexicanus*										U	1
Black-tailed Leafscraper — *S. caudacutus*										R	1
Sharp-tailed Streamcreeper — *Lochmias nematura*									R	R	7,11
ANTBIRDS — Formicariidae											
Fasciated Antshrike — *Cymbilaimus lineatus*										U	1,2
Undulated Antshrike — *Frederickena unduligera*										R	1,2
Great Antshrike — *Taraba major*		nU								F	3,5,6
Black-crested Antshrike — *Sakesphorus canadensis*										?	?
Collared Antshrike — *S. bernardi*		F									14,15,16
Barred Antshrike — *Thamnophilus doliatus*										F	3,5
Chapman's Antshrike — *T. zarumae*		U									3,15
Lined Antshrike — *T. palliatus*									F		3,7
Castelnau's Antshrike — *T. cryptoleucus*										nU	2
White-shouldered Antshrike — *T. aethiops*										U	1,2
Uniform Antshrike — *T. unicolor*								U			7
Black-capped Antshrike — *T. schistaceus*										F	1,2
Mouse-colored Antshrike — *T. murinus*										/F	1
Upland Antshrike — *T. aroyae*									s?		3
Slaty Antshrike — *T. punctatus*		cF									15,16
Amazonian Antshrike — *T. amazonicus*										U	2
Variable Antshrike — *T. caerulescens*								F			3,7
Rufous-capped Antshrike — *T. ruficapillus* Marcapata Antshrike — *T. marcapatae*								R			7
Spot-winged Antshrike — *Pygiptila stellaris*										F	1,2
Pearly Antshrike — *Megastictus margaritatus*										n?	?
Black Bushbird — *Neoctantes niger*										U	1
Russet Antshrike — *Thamnistes anabatinus*									U		7
Plain Antvireo — *Dysithamnus mentalis*		nF			nF			F	F	R	7,15

55

	WEST								EAST		
	sea and shore	arid tropical	arid subtropical	arid temperate	humid subtropical and temperate	puna	humid temperate	humid subtropical	humid upper tropical	humid tropical	habitats
Dusky-throated Antshrike — *Thamnomanes ardesiacus*										U	1,2
Saturnine Antshrike — *T. saturninus*										n?	?
Cinereous Antshrike — *T. caesius*										nF	1,2
Bluish-Slate Antshrike — *T. schistogynus*										sF	2
Pygmy Antwren — *Myrmotherula brachyura*										F	1,2
Short-billed Antwren — *M. obscura*									nU	nU	1
Sclater's Antwren — *M. sclateri*										lF	1,2
Streaked Antwren — *M. surinamensis*										U	6
Stripe-chested Antwren — *M. longicauda*									F		3
Plain-throated Antwren — *M. hauxwelli*										F	1,2
White-eyed Antwren — *M. leucophthalma*									U	F	1,2
Stipple-throated Antwren — *M. haematonota*										U	1
Ornate Antwren — *M. ornata*										U	2
Rufous-tailed Antwren — *M. erythrura*										U	1
White-flanked Antwren — *M. axillaris*										C	1,2
Slaty Antwren — *M. schisticolor*							F	C			7
Long-winged Antwren — *M. longipennis*										F	1,2
Rio Suno Antwren — *M. sunensis*										nR	1
Salvadori's Antwren — *M. minor*										n?	?
Ihering's Antwren — *M. iheringi*										sR	2
Gray Antwren — *M. menetriesii*										F	1,2
Leaden Antwren — *M. assimilis*										?	?
Banded Antbird — *Dichrozona cincta*										R	1,2
Black-capped Antwren — *Herpsilochmus pileatus*										?	?
Spot-tailed Antwren — *H. sticturus*										n?	?
Yellow-breasted Antwren — *H. axillaris*									R		7
Rufous-winged Antwren — *H. rufimarginatus*										lF	1,2
Dot-winged Antwren — *Microrhopias quixensis*										lF	1,2
Rusty-backed Antwren — *Formicivora rufa*										lF	4
Striated Antbird — *Drymophila devillei*										lF	2
Long-tailed Antbird — *D. caudata*								lF			7
Rufous-rumped Antwren — *Terenura callinota*									U		7
Chestnut-shouldered Antwren — *T. humeralis*										U	1,2
Yellow-rumped Antwren — *T. sharpei*									s?		7
Gray Antbird — *Cercomacra cinerascens*										F	1,2
Blackish Antbird — *C. nigrescens*									U	lU	3,5,7
Black Antbird — *C. serva*										R	3,5
Jet Antbird — *C. nigricans*										R	2

	sea and shore	arid tropical	arid subtropical	arid temperate	humid subtropical and temperate	puna	humid temperate	humid subtropical	humid upper tropical	humid tropical	habitats
Cercomacra — sp. nov.										s?	?
White-backed Fire-eye — *Pyriglena leuconota*		nF							F		3
White-browed Antbird — *Myrmoborus leucophrys*										C	1,2,3
Ash-breasted Antbird — *M. lugubris*										n?	2
Black-faced Antbird — *M. myotherinus*										C	1
Black-tailed Antbird — *M. melanurus*										F	2
Warbling Antbird — *Hypocnemis cantator*										C	1,2
Yellow-browed Antbird — *H. hypoxantha*										nU	1
Black-chinned Antbird — *Hypocnemoides melanopogon*										n?	2
Band-tailed Antbird — *H. maculicauda*										sU	2,6
Black-and-White Antbird — *Myrmochanes hemileucus*										nU	2
Black-headed Antbird — *Percnostola rufifrons*										n?	?
Slate-colored Antbird — *P. schistacea*										n?	?
Spot-winged Antbird — *P. leucostigma*									U	U	1,7
White-lined Antbird — *P. lophotes [=P. macrolopha]*										U	2
Silvered Antbird — *Sclateria naevia*										F	2,6
Chestnut-tailed Antbird — *Myrmeciza hemimelaena*										C	1,2
Plumbeous Antbird — *M. hyperythra*										F	2,6
White-shouldered Antbird — *M. melanoceps*										C	2
†Goeldi's Antbird — *M. goeldii*										sF	2
Sooty Antbird — *M. fortis*										lF	1
Gray-headed Antbird — *M. griseiceps*					U						7
Black-throated Antbird — *M. atrothorax*										C	3,5
White-plumed Antbird — *Pithys albifrons*										lF	1
White-masked Antbird — *P. castanea*										n?	?
White-throated Antbird — *Gymnopithys salvini*										F	1
Lunulated Antbird — *G. lunulata*										c?	1
Bicolored Antbird — *G. leucaspis*										nF	1
Hairy-crested Antbird — *Rhegmatorhina melanosticta*										U	1
Spot-backed Antbird — *Hylophylax naevia*									U	U	1,2
Dot-backed Antbird — *H. punctulata*										U	1
Scale-backed Antbird — *H. poecilonota*										lC	1
Black-spotted Bare-eye — *Phlegopsis nigromaculata*										U	1,2
Reddish-winged Bare-eye — *P. erythroptera*										U	?

	WEST								EAST		
	sea and shore	arid tropical	arid subtropical	arid temperate	humid subtropical and temperate	puna	humid temperate	humid subtropical	humid upper tropical	humid tropical	habitats
Short-tailed Antthrush — *Chamaeza campanisona*									U		7
Striated Antthrush — *C. nobilis*										R	1,2
Barred Antthrush — *C. mollissima*							R	R			7
Rufous-capped Antthrush — *Formicarius colma*										U	1
Black-faced Antthrush — *F. analis*										C	1,2
Rufous-fronted Antthrush — *F. rufifrons*										s?	?
Rufous-breasted Antthrush — *F. rufipectus*									R		7
Undulated Antpitta — *Grallaria squamigera*					R		U				7,8
Scaled Antpitta — *G. guatimalensis*									U		7
Ochre-striped Antpitta — *G. dignissima*										n?	1
Elusive Antpitta — *G. eludens*										/U	1
Chestnut-crowned Antpitta — *G. ruficapilla*			cF		F						3,7,15
Stripe-headed Antpitta — *G. andicola*				/F			R				9,13
Chestnut-naped Antpitta — *G. nuchalis*							nF				7
Grallaria — sp. nov.							cU				7
White-throated Antpitta — *G. albigula*								sF			?
Bay-backed (White-bellied) Antpitta — *G. hypoleuca*								nU			3,7
Rusty-tinged Antpitta — *G. przewalskii*								nF			3,7
Bay Antpitta — *G. capitalis*								cF			3,7
Red-and-White Antpitta — *G. erythroleuca*								sU			3,7
Rufous Antpitta — *G. rufula*					nF		F				7,8
Tawny Antpitta — *G. quitensis*					nF		nF				8,9
Spotted Antpitta — *Hylopezus macularius*										?	?
Fulvous-bellied Antpitta — *H. fulviventris*										nU	2,3
Amazonian Antpitta — *H. berlepschi*										R	2,3
Thrush-like Antpitta — *Myrmothera campanisona*										U	1,2
Ochre-breasted Antpitta — *Grallaricula flavirostris*								sU	U		7
Rusty-breasted Antpitta — *G. ferrugineipectus*					nR			F			7
Slate-crowned Antpitta — *G. nana*							nF				7,8
Grallaricula — sp. nov.								nR			7
Peruvian Antpitta — *G. peruviana*								nR			7
Ash-throated Gnateater — *Conopophaga peruviana*										R	1,2
Slaty Gnateater — *C. ardesiaca*								sU	sU		7
Chestnut-crowned Gnateater — *C. castaneiceps*								U	U		7
Chestnut-belted Gnateater — *C. aurita*										n?	1

			WEST					EAST			
	sea and shore	arid tropical	arid subtropical	arid temperate	humid subtropical and temperate	puna	humid temperate	humid subtropical	humid upper tropical	humid tropical	habitats
TAPACULOS — Rhinocryptidae											
Rusty-belted Tapaculo — *Liosceles thoracicus*										U	1
Marañón Crescentchest — *Melanopareia maranonica*		cU									15,16
Elegant Crescentchest — *M. elegans*		U									15,16
Ash-colored Tapaculo — *Myornis senilis*					nR		F				7
Unicolored Tapaculo — *Scytalopus unicolor*					nF		F	F			7
Large-footed Tapaculo — *S. macropus*							cU				7,11
Rufous-vented Tapaculo — *S. femoralis*								F	F		7
Brown-rumped Tapaculo — *S. latebricola*							nF				7
Andean Tapaculo — *S. magellanicus*				cF	?		C				8,9,13
Ocellated Tapaculo — *Acropternis orthonyx*							nR				7,8
COTINGAS — Cotingidae											
Black-necked Red-Cotinga — *Phoenicircus nigricollis*										n?	?
Shrike-like Cotinga — *Laniisoma elegans*									R	R	1,3,7
Red-crested Cotinga — *Ampelion rubrocristatus*			/F	F	U						8,12,13
Chestnut-crested Cotinga — *A. rufaxilla*								R			7
Bay-vented Cotinga — *A. [Doliornis] sclateri*							cR				8
White-cheeked Cotinga — *A. [Zaratornis] stresemanni*			/F	/U							13
Green-and-Black Fruiteater — *Pipreola riefferii*							F				7
Band-tailed Fruiteater — *P. intermedia*							F	U			7
Barred Fruiteater — *P. arcuata*							F	U			7,8
Golden-breasted Fruiteater — *P. aureopectus* †Black-chested Fruiteater — *P. lubomirskii*								nR			7
†Masked Fruiteater — *P. pulchra*								U			7
Scarlet-breasted Fruiteater — *P. frontalis*									U		7
Fiery-throated Fruiteater — *P. chlorolepidota*										R	1
Scaled Fruiteater — *Ampelioides tschudii*								U	R		7
White-browed Purpletuft — *Iodopleura isabellae*										R	3,5
Gray-tailed Piha — *Lipaugus subularis*									R		7
Olivaceous Piha — *L. cryptolophus*								U	U		7
Dusky Piha — *L. fuscocinereus*							nR				7
Screaming Piha — *L. vociferans*										C	1,2
Scimitar-winged Piha — *Chirocylla uropygialis*								sR			7
Purple-throated Cotinga — *Porphyrolaema porphyrolaema*										U	1
Plum-throated Cotinga — *Cotinga maynana*										U	1,2

	WEST							EAST			
	sea and shore	arid tropical	arid subtropical	arid temperate	humid subtropical and temperate	puna	humid temperate	humid subtropical	humid upper tropical	humid tropical	habitats
Spangled Cotinga — *C. cayana*										U	1,2
Black-faced Cotinga — *Conioptilon mcilhennyi*										/U	1,2
Bare-necked Fruitcrow — *Gymnoderus foetidus*										F	1,2
Purple-throated Fruitcrow — *Querula purpurata*										C	1,2
Red-ruffed Fruitcrow — *Pyroderus scutatus*								U	U		7
Amazonian Umbrellabird — *Cephalopterus ornatus*									U	/U	2,7
Andean Cock-of-the-Rock — *Rupicola peruviana*								U	U		7
MANAKINS — Pipridae											
Greater Manakin — *Schiffornis major*										U	2
Thrush-like Manakin — *S. turdinus*		nR							U	U	1
Wing-barred Manakin — *Piprites chloris*									U	U	1,2,7
Cinnamon Manakin — *Neopipo cinnamomea*										R	1
Green Manakin — *Chloropipo holochlora*										/F	1
Jet Manakin — *C. unicolor*								U	F		7
Black Manakin — *Xenopipo atronitens*										sR	3,4
Dwarf Tyrant-Manakin — *Tyranneutes stolzmanni*										F	1
Sulphur-bellied Tyrant-Manakin — *Neopelma sulphureiventer*										U	5
Orange-crowned Manakin — *Heterocercus aurantiivertex*										n?	?
Flame-crowned Manakin — *H. linteatus*										?	?
Striped Manakin — *Machaeropterus regulus*										nU	1
Fiery-capped Manakin — *M. pyrocephalus*										U	1,2
White-bearded Manakin — *Manacus manacus*		nR								/C	1
Golden-winged Manakin — *Masius chrysopterus*								nF	nF		7
Blue-backed Manakin — *Chiroxiphia pareola*									C	R	1,3,7
White-crowned Manakin — *Pipra pipra*								/C	/C	/C	1,7
Blue-crowned Manakin — *P. coronata*										F	1
Blue-rumped Manakin — *P. isidorei*									nR		7
Cerulean-capped Manakin — *P. coeruleocapilla*									F		7
Band-tailed Manakin — *P. fasciicauda*										F	2
Wire-tailed Manakin — *P. [Teleonema] filicauda*										nF	1,2
Golden-headed Manakin — *P. erythrocephala*										nF	1,2
Red-headed Manakin — *P. rubrocapilla*										/F	2
Round-tailed Manakin — *P. chloromeros*									/F	/F	1,2,7

TYRANT FLYCATCHERS — Tyrannidae

	WEST						EAST				
	sea and shore	arid tropical	arid subtropical	arid temperate	humid subtropical and temperate	puna	humid temperate	humid subtropical	humid upper tropical	humid tropical	habitats
Rough-legged Tyrannulet — *Phyllomyias [Acrochordopus] burmeisteri*									?		7
Sclater's Tyrannulet — *P. [Xanthomyias] sclateri*									sR		7
Sooty-headed Tyrannulet — *P. griseiceps*										R	1,3
Plumbeous-crowned Tyrannulet — *P. [Oreotriccus] plumbeiceps*								R			7
Black-capped Tyrannulet — *P. [Tyranniscus] nigrocapillus*					nR		U				7,8
Ashy-headed Tyrannulet — *P. [Tyranniscus] cinereiceps*								R			7
Tawny-rumped Tyrannulet — *P. [Tyranniscus] uropygialis*							U	U			7
Bolivian Tyrannulet — *Zimmerius [Tyranniscus] bolivianus*								sF			7
Red-billed Tyrannulet — *Z. [Tyranniscus] cinereicapillus*									?		?
Slender-footed Tyrannulet — *Z. [Tyranniscus] gracilipes*										F	1,2
Golden-faced Tyrannulet — *Z. [Tyranniscus] viridiflavus*					nR			cF	cF		7
White-lored Tyrannulet — *Ornithion inerme*										U	1,2
Southern Beardless Tyrannulet — *Camptostoma obsoletum*		C	F							U	3,16
Mouse-colored Tyrannulet — *Phaeomyias murina*		lC								R	3,14,16
Scrub Flycatcher — *Sublegatus modestus*										R	3
Todd's Flycatcher — *S. obscurior*										?	?
Yellow-crowned Tyrannulet — *Tyrannulus elatus*										F	2,3,5
Forest Elaenia — *Myiopagis gaimardii*										C	1,2
Gray Elaenia — *M. caniceps*										R	1,2
Pacific Elaenia — *M. subplacens*		U									15,16
Yellow-crowned Elaenia — *M. flavivertex*										lU	2
Greenish Elaenia — *M. viridicata*										U	2
Gray-and-White Tyrannulet — *M. [Phaeomyias] leucospodia*		F									14,16
Yellow-bellied Elaenia — *Elaenia flavogaster*		c?								U	3,5,6
Large Elaenia — *E. spectabilis*										U	5,6
White-crested Elaenia — *E. albiceps*					mF		mF	mC	m?	mR	3,12
Peruvian Elaenia — *E. modesta*			U								16
Small-billed Elaenia — *E. parvirostris*										U	3,5

| | WEST | | | | | | | EAST | | | |
Species	sea and shore	arid tropical	arid subtropical	arid temperate	humid subtropical and temperate	puna	humid temperate	humid subtropical	humid upper tropical	humid tropical	habitats
Slaty Elaenia — *E. strepera*								⌒		mU	2,5
Mottle-backed Elaenia — *E. gigas*									R		3
Brownish Elaenia — *E. pelzelni*										?	?
Plain-crested Elaenia — *E. cristata*										s?	?
Lesser Elaenia — *E. chiriquensis*			cU							lF	3,4
Highland Elaenia — *E. obscura*							F				3,7
Sierran Elaenia — *E. pallatangae*					F		C	F			3,7
White-throated Tyrannulet — *Mecocerculus leucophrys*					C		C				7,8
White-tailed Tyrannulet — *M. poecilocercus*								F			7
Buff-banded Tyrannulet — *M. hellmayri*								s?	s?		7
Rufous-winged Tyrannulet — *M. calopterus*		nR			nR			nR			7,15
Sulphur-bellied Tyrannulet — *M. minor*								F			3,7
White-banded Tyrannulet — *M. stictopterus*					nC		C				7
Torrent Tyrannulet — *Serpophaga cinerea*			R	R	R			F	U		11
River Tyrannulet — *S. hypoleuca*										R	5
Plain Tyrannulet — *Inezia inornata*										sU	5
Lesser Wagtail-Tyrant — *Stigmatura napensis*										n?	5
Ash-breasted Tit-Tyrant — *Anairetes alpinus*			lR				sR				13
Unstreaked Tit-Tyrant — *A. [Uromyias] agraphia*							R				7
Pied-crested Tit-Tyrant — *A. reguloides*			U								16
Black-crested Tit-Tyrant — *A. nigrocristatus*				lF							12,13
Yellow-billed Tit-Tyrant — *A. flavirostris*			F	F							12
Tufted Tit-Tyrant — *A. parulus*					F		U				8,13
Many-colored Rush-Tyrant — *Tachuris rubrigastra*	F					F					11,20
Subtropical Doradito — *Pseudocolopteryx acutipennis*								R		?	11
Tawny-crowned Pygmy-Tyrant — *Euscarthmus meloryphus*		C	U								14,15,16
Streak-necked Flycatcher — *Mionectes striaticollis*					U		R	F	U		3,7
Olive-striped Flycatcher — *M. olivaceus*									U	U	1,2,3
Ochre-bellied Flycatcher — *M. [Pipromorpha] oleagineus*		nU								F	1,2
McConnell's Flycatcher — *M. [Pipromorpha] macconnelli*									R	R	2,3
Rufous-breasted Flycatcher — *Leptopogon rufipectus*								nF			7
Inca Flycatcher — *L. taczanowskii*								F			7
Sepia-capped Flycatcher — *L. amaurocephalus*										U	1,2

	sea and shore	arid tropical	arid subtropical	arid temperate	humid subtropical and temperate	puna	humid temperate	humid subtropical	humid upper tropical	humid tropical	habitats
Slaty-capped Flycatcher — *L. superciliaris*					.				F		7
Variegated Bristle-Tyrant — *Phylloscartes [Pogonotriccus] poecilotis*								U			7
Marble-faced Bristle-Tyrant — *P. [Pogonotriccus] ophthalmicus*								U	F		7
Ecuadorean Bristle-Tyrant — *P. [Pogonotriccus] gualaquizae*								nR			7
Yellow-bellied Bristle-Tyrant — *P. [Pogonotriccus] flaviventris*									U		7
Spectacled Bristle-Tyrant — *P. [Pogonotriccus] orbitalis*									U		7
Mottle-cheeked Tyrannulet — *P. ventralis*								U			7
Bronze-Olive Pygmy-Tyrant — *Pseudotriccus pelzelni*								U	U		7
Hazel-fronted Pygmy-Tyrant — *P. simplex*								sU			7
Rufous-headed Pygmy-Tyrant — *P. ruficeps*							C				7
Ringed Antpipit — *Corythopis torquata*										F	1,2
Eared Pygmy-Tyrant — *Myiornis auricularis* White-breasted Pygmy-Tyrant — *M. albiventris*										U	15
Short-tailed Pygmy-Tyrant — *M. ecaudatus*										U	2,3
Scale-crested Pygmy-Tyrant — *Lophotriccus pileatus*				nF					F		7
Long-crested Pygmy-Tyrant — *L. eulophotes*										/R	2
Double-banded Pygmy-Tyrant — *L. vitiosus*										U	1,2
Rufous-crowned Tody-Tyrant — *Poecilotriccus ruficeps*								nR			7
Poecilotriccus — sp. nov.								nU			7
Black-and-White Tody-Flycatcher — *P. [Todirostrum] capitale*									nR	?	7
White-cheeked Tody-Flycatcher — *P. [Todirostrum] albifacies*										sR	2,5
Flammulated Pygmy-Tyrant — *Hemitriccus flammulatus*										/F	2
White-eyed Tody-Tyrant — *H. [Idioptilon] zosterops*										nU	1,2
White-bellied Tody-Tyrant — *H. [Idioptilon] griseipectus*										sF	1,2
Johannis' Tody-Tyrant — *H. [Idioptilon] iohannis*										U	2,5
Stripe-necked Tody-Tyrant — *H. [Idioptilon] striaticollis*										/U	4,5
Pearly-vented Tody-Tyrant — *H. [Idioptilon] margaritaceiventer*										sU	4

	WEST							EAST			
	sea and shore	arid tropical	arid subtropical	arid temperate	humid subtropical and temperate	puna	humid temperate	humid subtropical	humid upper tropical	humid tropical	habitats
Black-throated Tody-Tyrant — H. [Idioptilon] granadensis							U				3,7
Buff-throated Tody-Tyrant — H. [Idioptilon] rufigularis									/F		7
Cinnamon-breasted Tody-Tyrant — H. cinnamomeipectus								nR			7
Ochre-faced Tody-Flycatcher — Todirostrum plumbeiceps								sF	s?		3
Rusty-fronted Tody-Flycatcher — T. latirostre										F	3,5
Spotted Tody-Flycatcher — T. maculatum										U	5,6
Common Tody-Flycather — T. cinereum		F								U	3,15,16
Painted Tody-Flycatcher — T. chrysocrotaphum										F	2,3
Golden-winged Tody-Flycatcher — T. calopterum									U	U	3
Brownish Flycatcher — Cnipodectes subbrunneus										U	1
Large-headed Flatbill — Ramphotrigon megacephala										/F	2
Dusky-tailed Flatbill — R. fuscicauda										R	2
Rufous-tailed Flatbill — R. ruficauda										U	1,2
Olivaceous Flatbill — Rhynchocyclus olivaceus										U	2
Fulvous-breasted Flatbill — R. fulvipectus									U		7
Yellow-Olive Flycatcher — Tolmomyias sulphurescens		nU							U	?	7,15
Yellow-margined Flycatcher — T. assimilis										F	1,2
Gray-crowned Flycatcher — T. poliocephalus										U	1,2
Yellow-breasted Flycatcher — T. flaviventris										F	3,5
Cinnamon-crested Spadebill — Platyrinchus saturatus										n?	1
White-throated Spadebill — P. mystaceus								U	F		3,7
Golden-crowned Spadebill — P. coronatus										U	1,2
Yellow-throated Spadebill — P. flavigularis								nR			7
White-crested Spadebill — P. platyrhynchos										R	1,2
Royal Flycatcher — Onychorhynchus coronatus		nU								U	1,2,15
Ornate Flycatcher — Myiotriccus ornatus									F		7
Ruddy-tailed Flycatcher — Terenotriccus erythrurus										F	1,2
Tawny-breasted Flycatcher — Myiobius villosus									U		7
Sulphur-rumped Flycatcher — M. barbatus										U	1
Black-tailed Flycatcher — M. atricaudus		nF								U	1,15
Flavescent Flycatcher — Myiophobus flavicans								U			7
Orange-crested Flycatcher — M. phoenicomitra									nU		7

Species	sea and shore	arid tropical	arid subtropical	arid temperate	humid subtropical and temperate	puna	humid temperate	humid subtropical	humid upper tropical	humid tropical	habitats
		WEST						EAST			
Unadorned Flycatcher — *M. inornatus*								sU			7
Roraiman Flycatcher — *M. roraimae*									R		7
Orange-banded Flycatcher — *M. lintoni*							nU				7
Handsome Flycatcher — *M. pulcher*							s?	s?			7
Ochraceous-breasted Flycatcher — *M. ochraceiventris*							F				7,8
Olive-chested Flycatcher — *M. cryptoxanthus*									nR		3,7
Bran-colored Flycatcher — *M. fasciatus*		F	U						U	U	3,6,16
Cinnamon Flycatcher — *Pyrrhomyias cinnamomea*							U	C			7
Olive Flycatcher — *Mitrephanes olivaceus*							R	U			7
Olive-sided Flycatcher — *Contopus [Nuttallornis] borealis*							mR	mR	mR		6,7
Greater Pewee — *C. fumigatus*		R		U			F	F			7
Western Wood Pewee — *C. sordidulus*				m?							?
Eastern Wood Pewee — *C. virens*										mF	2,3,5
Tropical Pewee — *C. cinereus*		F	U	U							15
Blackish Pewee — *C. nigrescens*									R		7
Alder Flycatcher — *Empidonax alnorum*							mR	mU	mF		3,5,6
Euler's Flycatcher — *E. euleri*									U	F	1,7
Gray-breasted Flycatcher — *E. griseipectus*		U									15
Fuscous Flycatcher — *Cnemotriccus fuscatus*										R	3,5
Black Phoebe — *Sayornis nigricans* / White-winged Phoebe — *S. latirostris*	R	U	U	U				F	F		11
Vermilion Flycatcher — *Pyrocephalus rubinus*	C	C								U	+
Slaty-backed Chat-Tyrant — *Ochthoeca cinnamomeiventris*								U			7
Yellow-bellied Chat-Tyrant — *O. diadema*							nU				7
Crowned Chat-Tyrant — *O. frontalis*							F				8
Golden-browed Chat-Tyrant — *O. pulchella*				U			U	U			7,8,13
Rufous-breasted Chat-Tyrant — *O. rufipectoralis*				/U	F		C	U			7,13
Brown-backed Chat-Tyrant — *O. fumicolor*					F		C				9
d'Orbigny's Chat-Tyrant — *O. oenanthoides*				F							12,13
White-browed Chat-Tyrant — *O. leucophrys*			F	C							12,13
Piura Chat-Tyrant — *O. piurae*		nR	nU								12,16
Drab Water-Tyrant — *O. [Ochthornis] littoralis*										C	5
Streak-throated Bush-Tyrant — *Myiotheretes striaticollis*			U	F	U		U	U			3,12
Red-rumped Bush-Tyrant — *M. erythropygius*							U				9
Rufous-webbed Tyrant — *M. [Xolmis] rufipennis*				/U							12,13

Species	sea and shore	arid tropical	arid subtropical	arid temperate	humid subtropical and temperate	puna	humid temperate	humid subtropical	humid upper tropical	humid tropical	habitats
Smoky Bush-Tyrant — *M. fumigatus*							U				7,8
Rufous-bellied Bush-Tyrant — *M. fuscorufus*							sR	sR			3,7
Gray Monjita — *Xolmis cinerea*										sF	4
Black-billed Shrike-Tyrant — *Agriornis montana*			R	F		U					10,12
White-tailed Shrike-Tyrant — *A. andicola [=A. albicauda]*				U							12
Gray-bellied Shrike-Tyrant — *A. microptera*				s?		s?					12
Spot-billed Ground-Tyrant — *Muscisaxicola maculirostris*				F							12
Little Ground-Tyrant — *M. fluviatilis*										U	5
Dark-faced Ground-Tyrant — *M. macloviana*	mU		mU								17,19,21
Cinnamon-bellied Ground-Tyrant — *M. capistrata*						mU					10
Rufous-naped Ground-Tyrant — *M. rufivertex*			sU	F		C					10,12
Puna Ground-Tyrant — *M. juninensis*						C					10
White-browed Ground-Tyrant — *M. albilora*						mF					10
Plain-capped Ground-Tyrant — *M. alpina*				F		F					9,10,12
Cinereous Ground-Tyrant — *M. cinerea*				mU		mU					10,12
White-fronted Ground-Tyrant — *M. albifrons*						F					10
Ochre-naped Ground-Tyrant — *M. flavinucha*						mF					10
Black-fronted Ground-Tyrant — *M. frontalis*						mR					10
Andean Rufous-backed Negrito — *Lessonia oreas*	mR					C					11
Amazonian Black-Tyrant — *Knipolegus [Phaeotriccus] poecilocercus*										R	5
Plumbeous Tyrant — *K. signatus [=Myiotheretes signatus]*							R	R			3,7
Rufous-tailed Tyrant — *K. poecilurus*								U			3
Riverside Tyrant — *K. orenocensis*										U	5
White-winged Black-Tyrant — *K. aterrimus*			cU	lU				lU			3,12
*Spectacled Tyrant — *Hymenops perspicillata*								mR			11
Pied Water-Tyrant — *Fluvicola pica*										mU	5,6
Masked Water-Tyrant — *F. nengeta*		nU									5
White-headed Marsh-Tyrant — *F. [Arundinicola] leucocephala*										U	5
Long-tailed Tyrant — *Colonia colonus*									F	U	3
Yellow-browed Tyrant — *Satrapa icterophrys*										mU	3,5
Tumbes Tyrant — *Tumbezia salvini*		F									14, 15, 16
Short-tailed Field-Tyrant — *Muscigralla brevicauda*		F	U								14,17
Cliff Flycatcher — *Hirundinea ferruginea*								lF	lF	lF	3

	WEST							EAST			
	sea and shore	arid tropical	arid subtropical	arid temperate	humid subtropical and temperate	puna	humid temperate	humid subtropical	humid upper tropical	humid tropical	habitats
Cinnamon Attila — *Attila cinnamomeus*										?	2
Citron-bellied Attila — *A. citriniventris*										n?	?
Dull-capped Attila — *A. bolivianus*										U	2
Bright-rumped Attila — *A. spadiceus*										F	1,2
Rufous Casiornis — *Casiornis rufa*										sR	5
Grayish Mourner — *Rhytipterna simplex*										F	1,2
Cinereous Mourner — *Laniocera hypopyrra*										U	1
Sirystes — *Sirystes sibilator*										F	2,3
Rufous Flycatcher — *Myiarchus semirufus*		lF									14
Dusky-capped Flycatcher — *M. tuberculifer*			U	U	F			F	U	R	7,16
Swainson's Flycatcher — *M. swainsoni*										U	1,2
Short-crested Flycatcher — *M. ferox*										F	3,5
Pale-edged Flycatcher — *M. cephalotes*								U			3
Sooty-crowned Flycatcher — *M. phaeocephalus*		U									15
Brown-crested Flycatcher — *M. tyrannulus*		cF									14,16
Lesser Kiskadee — *Pitangus lictor*										F	6
Great Kiskadee — *P. sulphuratus*										C	3,5,6
Boat-billed Flycatcher — *Megarhynchus pitangua*										F	3,5,6
*Rusty-margined Flycatcher — *Myiozetetes cayanensis*										sU	6
Social Flycatcher — *M. similis*		lF								C	3,5,6
Gray-capped Flycatcher — *M. granadensis*		n?								C	3,5,6
Dusky-chested Flycatcher — *M. [Tyrannopsis] luteiventris*										R	2,3
*White-ringed Flycatcher — *Conopias parva*										n?	?
Three-striped Flycatcher — *C. trivirgata*										R	2
Lemon-browed Flycatcher — *C. cinchoneti*									U		7
Golden-crowned Flycatcher — *Myiodynastes chrysocephalus*								U	U		3,7
Baird's Flycatcher — *M. bairdii*		C									14,15,16
Streaked Flycatcher — *M. maculatus*		F							F	F	1,2,15
Sulphur-bellied Flycatcher — *M. luteiventris*										mF	1,2
Piratic Flycatcher — *Legatus leucophaius*										lC	1,2
Variegated Flycatcher — *Empidonomus varius*										lC	1,2
Crowned Slaty-Flycatcher — *E. aurantioatrocristatus*										mU	3,5
Sulphury Flycatcher — *Tyrannopsis sulphurea*										sU	4,6
Snowy-throated Kingbird — *Tyrannus niveigularis*		lU									14,15,16

67

	sea and shore	arid tropical	arid subtropical	arid temperate	humid subtropical and temperate	puna	humid temperate	humid subtropical	humid upper tropical	humid tropical	habitats
White-throated Kingbird — *T. albogularis*										lF	3,5
Tropical Kingbird — *T. melancholicus*		lF	lF					U	C	C	+
Fork-tailed Flycatcher — *T. savana [=Muscivora tyrannus]*										mU	3,5,6
Eastern Kingbird — *T. tyrannus*			mR					mR	m?	mC	2,3,5
Green-backed Becard — *Pachyramphus viridis*									U	U	1
Barred Becard — *P. versicolor*							F	F	F		7
Slaty Becard — *P. spodiurus*		U									15
Cinereous Becard — *P. rufus*										R	?
Chestnut-crowned Becard — *P. castaneus*										R	1,2
White-winged Becard — *P. polychopterus*										F	3,5
Black-capped Becard — *P. marginatus*										U	1,2
Black-and-White Becard — *P. albogriseus*		U		U				U	U		7,15,16
One-colored Becard — *P. [Platypsaris] homochrous*		nF									15
Pink-throated Becard — *P. [Platypsaris] minor*										U	1,2
Crested Becard — *P. validus [=Platypsaris rufus]*										?	?
Black-tailed Tityra — *Tityra cayana*										U	1,2
Masked Tityra — *T. semifasciata*									U	F	1,2,3
Black-crowned Tityra — *T. inquisitor*										U	2
SHARPBILLS — Oxyruncidae											
Sharpbill — *Oxyruncus cristatus*									R		7
PLANTCUTTERS — Phytotomidae											
Peruvian Plantcutter — *Phytotoma raimondii*		lF									14,16
SWALLOWS — Hirundinidae											
Mangrove Swallow — *Tachycineta albilinea*		lF									16,17
White-winged Swallow — *T. albiventer*										C	5,6
White-rumped Swallow — *T. leucorrhoa*										mR	?
*Chilean Swallow — *T. leucopyga*			mR								?
Brown-chested Martin — *Phaeoprogne tapera*										U	5,6
Purple Martin — *Progne subis*										mR	3
Gray-breasted Martin — *P. chalybea*		lF								F	3,5
Southern Martin — *P. modesta*	R									mC	17
Brown-bellied Swallow — *Notiochelidon murina*				C			C				9,12
Blue-and-White Swallow — *N. cyanoleuca*			C	C	F		F	C	F	R	+
Pale-footed Swallow — *N. flavipes*							lC				7,8
White-banded Swallow — *Atticora fasciata*										C	3,5

	sea and shore	arid tropical	arid subtropical	arid temperate	humid subtropical and temperate	puna	humid temperate	humid subtropical	humid upper tropical	humid tropical	habitats
White-thighed Swallow — *Neochelidon tibialis*										/F	1,3
Tawny-headed Swallow — *Alopochelidon fucata*										m?	?
Rough-winged Swallow — *Stelgidopteryx ruficollis*		cF							F	C	3,5
Bank Swallow — *Riparia riparia*		mR	mR							mR	3,20
Barn Swallow — *Hirundo rustica*		mR	mU	mU		mU	mU			mU	+
Andean Swallow — *Petrochelidon andecola*				U		C					10,12
*Cliff Swallow — *P. pyrrhonota*		mR	mR								17,20
Cave Swallow — *P. fulva*		/C	/U								17
JAYS — Corvidae											
Collared Jay — *Cyanolyca viridicyana*							F				7
Turquoise Jay — *C. turcosa*				F			nF				7
Purplish Jay — *Cyanocorax cyanomelas*									sC		3,5
Violaceous Jay — *C. violaceus*										C	2,3,5
White-tailed Jay — *C. mystacalis*		C									15,16
Green Jay — *C. yncas*		cF	cC					F	F		7,15,16
DIPPERS — Cinclidae											
White-capped Dipper — *Cinclus leucocephalus*			U	U	U		U	U	U		11
WRENS — Troglodytidae											
Thrush-like Wren — *Campylorhynchus turdinus*										F	3,6
Fasciated Wren — *C. fasciatus*		C	U								12,14,15
Gray-mantled Wren — *Odontorchilus branickii*								U	U		7
Rufous Wren — *Cinnycerthia unirufa*							nC				7,8
Sepia-Brown Wren — *C. peruana*							C				7
Sedge Wren — *Cistothorus platensis*					/U		C				9
Plain-tailed Wren — *Thryothorus euophrys*							/C	/C			3,7
Thryothorus — sp. nov.							sF				7
Moustached Wren — *T. genibarbis*									/F	/F	3,5,6
Coraya Wren — *T. coraya*										/F	3
Spot-breasted Wren — *T. maculipectus*		F	cF								15,16
Buff-breasted Wren — *T. leucotis*										/C	3,5
Superciliated Wren — *T. superciliaris*		C									14,15,16
House Wren — *Troglodytes aedon*		U	C	C	F	F	F	F	F	F	3,12,17
Mountain Wren — *T. solstitialis*					U		C	C			3,7
White-breasted Wood-Wren — *Henicorhina leucosticta*										/C	1

	WEST							EAST			
	sea and shore	arid tropical	arid subtropical	arid temperate	humid subtropical and temperate	puna	humid temperate	humid subtropical	humid upper tropical	humid tropical	habitats
Gray-breasted Wood-Wren — *H. leucophrys*					nF			C	C		7
Bar-winged Wood-Wren — *H. leucoptera*								nF			8
Nightingale Wren — *Microcerculus marginatus*										C	1,2
Wing-banded Wren — *M. bambla*										R	1,2
Chestnut-breasted Wren — *Cyphorhinus thoracicus*								U	U		7
Musician Wren — *C. arada*										F	1,2
MOCKINGBIRDS AND THRASHERS — Mimidae											
Long-tailed Mockingbird — *Mimus longicaudatus*		C	lC								14,16
Black-capped Mockingthrush — *Donacobius atricapillus*										C	6
THRUSHES AND SOLITAIRES — Turdidae											
Andean Solitaire — *Myadestes ralloides*								C	F		7
Rufous-Brown Solitaire — *M. leucogenys*									R		7
White-eared Solitaire — *Entomodestes leucotis*							R	F	U		7
Slaty-backed Nightingale-Thrush — *Catharus fuscater*					U			U			7
Spotted Nightingale-Thrush — *C. dryas*					nU				U		7
*Veery — *C. fuscescens*										mR	?
Gray-cheeked Thrush — *C. minimus*										mR	?
Swainson's Thrush — *C. ustulatus*		mR	mR					mF	mF	mU	+
Pale-eyed Thrush — *Platycichla leucops*								U	U		7
Chiguanco Thrush — *Turdus chiguanco*			U	C			R				3,12,17
Great Thrush — *T. fuscater*				lF	C		C	F			7,13
Glossy-Black Thrush — *T. serranus*					U		F	F			7
Slaty Thrush — *T. nigriceps*					R			R	R	R	1,7
Plumbeous-backed Thrush — *T. reevei*		F									15,16
Marañón Thrush — *T. maranonicus*		cF	cU								15,16
Chestnut-bellied Thrush — *T. fulviventris*								nU	nU		3,7
Pale-breasted Thrush — *T. leucomelas*										sU	4
Creamy-bellied Thrush — *T. amaurochalinus*										sF	2,3,5
Black-billed Thrush — *T. ignobilis*										C	3,5
Lawrence's Thrush — *T. lawrencii*										lF	2
Pale-vented Thrush — *T. obsoletus* Hauxwell's Thrush — *T. hauxwelli*										U	1,2
Bare-eyed Thrush — *T. nudigenis*		nF									15
White-necked Thrush — *T. albicollis*									U	F	1,2

	sea and shore	arid tropical	arid subtropical	arid temperate	humid subtropical and temperate	puna	humid temperate	humid subtropical	humid upper tropical	humid tropical	habitats
GNATWRENS AND GNATCATCHERS — Sylviidae											
Half-collared Gnatwren — *Microbates cinereiventris*										U	1
Long-billed Gnatwren — *Ramphocaenus melanurus*		nU								U	1,2,15
Tropical Gnatcatcher — *Polioptila plumbea*		C	lU							R	3,12,14
PIPITS — Motacillidae											
Short-billed Pipit — *Anthus furcatus*						F					10
Hellmayr's Pipit — *A. hellmayri*					sF	?					?
Yellowish Pipit — *A. lutescens*	F		C								20
Correndera Pipit — *A. correndera*						F					10
Paramo Pipit — *A. bogotensis*					F	U	F				9,10
WEAVER FINCHES — Ploceidae											
House Sparrow — *Passer domesticus*		iU	iC								17
VIREOS — Vireonidae											
Rufous-browed Peppershrike — *Cyclarhis gujanensis*		cU			U			F	F	lF	3,7,15
Slaty-capped Shrike-Vireo — *Smaragdolanius leucotis*									lC	R	1,7
Red-eyed Vireo — *Vireo olivaceus*		nU								F	1,2
Black-whiskered Vireo — *V. altiloquus*										n?	?
Warbling Vireo — *V. gilvus*					U		C	C			7
Lemon-chested Greenlet — *Hylophilus thoracicus*										F	1,2
Dusky-capped Greenlet — *H. hypoxanthus*										C	1,2
Olivaceous Greenlet — *H. olivaceus*									F		7
Tawny-crowned Greenlet — *H. ochraceiceps*										lF	1,2
Lesser Greenlet — *H. minor*		nF									15
AMERICAN ORIOLES AND BLACKBIRDS — Icteridae											
Shiny Cowbird — *Molothrus bonariensis*		lC								R	3,16,17
Giant Cowbird — *Scaphidura oryzivora*										C	3,5,6
Band-tailed Oropendola — *Ocyalus latirostris*										nF	2
Casqued Oropendola — *Clypicterus oseryi*										lF	1,2
Crested Oropendola — *Psarocolius decumanus*									U	C	1,2,3
Green Oropendola — *P. viridis*										n?	2
Dusky-Green Oropendola — *P. atrovirens*								F	U		3,7
Russet-backed Oropendola — *P. angustifrons*									F	C	2,3,5
Olive Oropendola — *Gymnostinops yuracares*										lC	1,2
Yellow-rumped Cacique — *Cacicus cela*		nR								C	+

	sea and shore	arid tropical	arid subtropical	arid temperate	humid subtropical and temperate	puna	humid temperate	humid subtropical	humid upper tropical	humid tropical	habitats
Red-rumped Cacique — *C. haemorrhous*										R	2,3,5
Scarlet-rumped Cacique — *C. uropygialis*								U			7
Selva Cacique — *C. koepckeae*										/R	2
Mountain Cacique — *C. leucorhamphus*							F				7
Ecuadorean Black Cacique — *C. sclateri*										nU	3,5
Solitary Black Cacique — *C. solitarius*										U	2,5
Yellow-billed Cacique — *C. holosericeus*		nU					F				7,15
Scrub Blackbird — *Dives warszewiczi*		C	/C	U							16,17
Great-tailed Grackle — *Quiscalus [Cassidix] mexicanus*	nF										18
Velvet-fronted Grackle — *Lampropsar tanagrinus*										/U	2
Chopi Blackbird — *Gnorimopsar chopi*										sU	4
Yellow-winged Blackbird — *Agelaius thilius*						sC					11
Pale-eyed Blackbird — *A. xanthophthalmus*										/U	6
Yellow-hooded Blackbird — *A. icterocephalus*	iR									nU	5,6
Epaulet Oriole — *Icterus cayanensis*									U	C	3,5,6
†Moriche Oriole — *I. chrysocephalus*										U	3,5,6
Troupial — *I. icterus*										F	3,6
White-edged Oriole — *I. graceannae*		C									14,15,16
Yellow-tailed Oriole — *I. mesomelas*		U									15
Oriole Blackbird — *Gymnomystax mexicanus*										/U	3,6
Red-breasted Blackbird — *Leistes militaris*										n?	3,6
White-browed Blackbird — *L. superciliaris*										s?	?
Peruvian Red-breasted Meadowlark — *Sturnella bellicosa*		C	C								12,14,17
Bobolink — *Dolichonyx oryzivorus*			mR							mU	3

WOOD WARBLERS — Parulidae

	sea and shore	arid tropical	arid subtropical	arid temperate	humid subtropical and temperate	puna	humid temperate	humid subtropical	humid upper tropical	humid tropical	habitats
*Black-and-White Warbler — *Mniotilta varia*		mR						mR			7,16
Tropical Parula — *Parula pitiayumi*		F			F			F	C		7,15
Yellow Warbler — *Dendroica petechia*										mR	+
Mangrove Warbler — *D. erithachorides*	nF										18
Cerulean Warbler — *D. cerulea*										m?	?
Blackburnian Warbler — *D. fusca*					mF		mF	mC	m?	mR	1,2,7
Blackpoll Warbler — *D. striata*										mU	1,2
Northern Waterthrush — *Seiurus noveboracensis*										m?	?
Masked Yellowthroat — *Geothlypis aequinoctialis*		U	F							U	5,12,16
Connecticut Warbler — *Oporornis agilis*										mR	3
Canada Warbler — *Wilsonia canadensis*								mF	m?	m?	3,7
American Redstart — *Setophaga ruticilla*		mR	mR							mR	3,16

	sea and shore	arid tropical	arid subtropical	arid temperate	humid subtropical and temperate	puna	humid temperate	humid subtropical	humid upper tropical	humid tropical	habitats
Slate-throated Redstart — *Myioborus miniatus*					F			C	C		7
Spectacled Redstart — *M. melanocephalus*					F		C	F			7,8
Black-crested Warbler — *Basileuterus nigrocristatus*				/F	C		nC	nU			3,7,9
Citrine Warbler — *B. luteoviridis*							C	F			7,8
Pale-legged Warbler — *B. signatus*								sF			3,7
Two-banded Warbler — *B. bivittatus*									sC		3
Golden-bellied Warbler — *B. chrysogaster*										R	1
Three-striped Warbler — *B. tristriatus*								F	C		3,7
Three-banded Warbler — *B. trifasciatus*		F			C						3,7,15
Russet-crowned Warbler — *B. coronatus*					C			C	F		7
Gray-and-Gold Warbler — *B. fraseri*		F			U						15,16
River Warbler — *B. rivularis*										F	2,5
HONEYCREEPERS — Coerebidae											
Bananaquit — *Coereba flaveola*		/C							/C	/?	3,14,16
Chestnut-vented Conebill — *Conirostrum speciosum*										/F	2,3,5
Bicolored Conebill — *C. bicolor*										n?	?
Pearly-breasted Conebill — *C. margaritae*										n?	?
Cinereous Conebill — *C. cinereum*		F	C	C	F		U				+
Tamarugo Conebill — *C. tamarugensis*				sF							12,13
White-browed Conebill — *C. ferrugineiventre*							F				8,9
Blue-backed Conebill — *C. sitticolor*					F		C				7,8
Capped Conebill — *C. albifrons*								F			7
Giant Conebill — *Oreomanes fraseri*				/F							13
Bluish Flower-piercer — *Diglossa caerulescens*								F			7
Slaty Flowerpiercer — *D. baritula* / Rusty Flower-piercer — *D. sittoides*			U	U	U		R	R			3,7,12
Glossy Flower-piercer — *D. lafresnayii*							nC				8,9
Moustached Flower-piercer — *D. mystacalis*							C				8,9
Carbonated Flower-piercer — *D. carbonaria* / Black Flower-piercer — *D. humeralis*					nC		nC				3,9
Black-throated Flower-piercer — *D. brunneiventris*				F			C				+
White-sided Flower-piercer — *D. albilatera*					nU			nC			3
Deep-Blue Flower-piercer — *D. glauca*									F		7
Masked Flower-piercer — *D. cyanea*					F		C	C			7,8
Short-billed Honeycreeper — *Cyanerpes nitidus*										?	?
Purple Honeycreeper — *C. caeruleus*										C	1,2
Red-legged Honeycreeper — *C. cyaneus*										U	1,2
Green Honeycreeper — *Chlorophanes spiza*									U	C	1,2

	sea and shore	arid tropical	arid subtropical	arid temperate	humid subtropical and temperate	puna	humid temperate	humid subtropical	humid upper tropical	humid tropical	habitats
Golden-collared Honeycreeper — *Iridophanes pulcherrima*								U	U		3,7
Blue Dacnis — *Dacnis cayana*									U	C	1,2
Black-faced Dacnis — *D. lineata*									U	C	1,2
Yellow-bellied Dacnis — *D. flaviventer*									R	R	2,3
White-bellied Dacnis — *D. albiventris*										R	3?
Tit-like Dacnis — *Xenodacnis parina*			lC				sU				12,13
O'Neill's Pardusco — *Nephelornis oneilli*							cF				8,9
SWALLOW-TANAGERS — Tersinidae											
Swallow-Tanager — *Tersina viridis*										lF	3,5
TANAGERS — Thraupidae											
Blue-naped Chlorophonia — *Chlorophonia cyanea*								U	C	R	1,7
Chestnut-breasted Chlorophonia — *C. pyrrhophrys*								U			7
Blue-hooded Euphonia — *Euphonia musica*				C				U			3,7
Orange-bellied Euphonia — *E. xanthogaster*		nU						U	C	F	1,2,7
White-vented Euphonia — *E. minuta*										F	2,3
Orange-crowned Euphonia — *E. saturata*		nR									3
Purple-throated Euphonia — *E. chlorotica*		cC								lC	3,5,16
Thick-billed Euphonia — *E. laniirostris*		F								lF	3,5
Rufous-bellied Euphonia — *E. rufiventris*										F	1,2,3
Bronze-Green Euphonia — *E. mesochrysa*									U		7
Golden-bellied Euphonia — *E. chrysopasta*										F	2,3,5
Fawn-breasted Tanager — *Pipraeidea melanonota*		R	R	R				R	R	?	3
Orange-eared Tanager — *Chlorochrysa calliparaea*									F		7
Opal-rumped Tanager — *Tangara velia*										U	1,2
Opal-crowned Tanager — *T. callophrys*										U	1,2
Paradise Tanager — *T. chilensis*									U	C	1,2
Green-and-Gold Tanager — *T. schrankii*									U	C	1,2
Spotted Tanager — *T. punctata*									F		7
Yellow-bellied Tanager — *T. xanthogastra*										U	1,2
Golden Tanager — *T. arthus*									F		7
Saffron-crowned Tanager — *T. xanthocephala*								C	U		7
Golden-eared Tanager — *T. chrysotis*									U		7
Flame-faced Tanager — *T. parzudakii*								C	U		7
Blue-browed Tanager — *T. cyanotis*								U	U		7
Metallic-Green Tanager — *T. labradorides*								nU			7
Blue-necked Tanager — *T. cyanicollis*								R	C	U	7
Masked Tanager — *T. nigrocincta*										F	1,2

| | WEST | | | | | | EAST | | | | |
	sea and shore	arid tropical	arid subtropical	arid temperate	humid subtropical and temperate	puna	humid temperate	humid subtropical	humid upper tropical	humid tropical	habitats
Golden-naped Tanager — *T. ruficervix*								U			7
Turquoise Tanager — *T. mexicana*										F	1,2,3
Bay-headed Tanager — *T. gyrola*		nF							F	U	1,3,7
Burnished-Buff Tanager — *T. cayana*										lC	4
Beryl-spangled Tanager — *T. nigroviridis*								C	U		7
Blue-and-Black Tanager — *T. vassorii*					U		U	C			7
Black-capped Tanager — *T. heinei*								l?			7
Silvery Tanager — *T. viridicollis*			cF		F			F			7
Green-throated Tanager — *T. argyrofenges*								nU			7
Yellow-throated Tanager — *Iridosornis analis*								U	U		7
Golden-collared Tanager — *I. jelskii*							U				8
Golden-crowned Tanager — *I. rufivertex*							nF				7,8
†Yellow-scarfed Tanager — *I. reinhardti*							F				7
Scarlet-bellied Mountain-Tanager — *Anisognathus igniventris*					R		C	R			7,8
Lacrimose Mountain-Tanager — *A. lacrymosus*							C	U			7,8
Blue-winged Mountain-Tanager — *A. flavinucha*								C	F		7
Hooded Mountain-Tanager — *Buthraupis montana*							C	U			7
Black-chested Mountain-Tanager — *B. eximia*							nU				8
Golden-backed Mountain-Tanager — *B. aureodorsalis*							cU				8
Masked Mountain-Tanager — *B. wetmorei*							nR				8
Orange-throated Tanager — *Wetmorethraupis sterrhopteron*									nU	nU	1,7
Chestnut-bellied Mountain-Tanager — *Dubusia castaneoventris*							U				8
Buff-breasted Mountain-Tanager — *D. taeniata*							U	U			7,8
Blue-Gray Tanager — *Thraupis episcopus*	U	iU						R	U	C	3,5,6
*Sayaca Tanager — *T. sayaca*										sR	3,4?
Palm Tanager — *T. palmarum*									C	C	7
Blue-capped Tanager — *T. cyanocephala*					C			C			7
Blue-and-Yellow Tanager — *T. bonariensis*			C	C	F		U	R			12,17
Silver-beaked Tanager — *Ramphocelus carbo*									C	C	3,5,6
Black-bellied Tanager — *R. melanogaster*								cU	cU	cC	3
Masked Crimson Tanager — *R. nigrogularis*									R	F	3,6
Vermilion Tanager — *Calochaetes coccineus*								U	U		7
Hepatic Tanager — *Piranga flava*			U	U			R	R			7,12
Summer Tanager — *P. rubra*				mR				mU	m?	mU	+
Scarlet Tanager — *P. olivacea*										mU	1,2
White-winged Tanager — *P. leucoptera*									F		7
Red-hooded Tanager — *P. rubriceps*								U			7

75

	WEST								EAST		
	sea and shore	arid tropical	arid subtropical	arid temperate	humid subtropical and temperate	puna	humid temperate	humid subtropical	humid upper tropical	humid tropical	habitats
Carmiol's Tanager — *Chlorothraupis carmioli*									lC	lC	1
Red-crowned Ant-Tanager — *Habia rubica*										C	1,2
Fulvous Shrike-Tanager — *Lanio fulvus*									nU	n?	1,7
White-winged Shrike-Tanager — *L. versicolor*										F	1,2
White-lined Tanager — *Tachyphonus rufus*										lC	3
Flame-crested Tanager — *T. cristatus*										F	1,2
Fulvous-crested Tanager — *T. surinamus*										lF	1
Red-shouldered Tanager — *T. phoenicius*										lC	4
Yellow-crested Tanager — *T. rufiventer*									U	F	1
White-shouldered Tanager — *T. luctuosus*									U	F	1,2,7
Rufous-crested Tanager — *Creurgops verticalis*								U	U		7
Slaty Tanager — *C. dentata*								sU			7
Gray-headed Tanager — *Eucometis penicillata*										lF	2
Black-goggled Tanager — *Trichothraupis melanops*									U		3,7
Hooded Tanager — *Nemosia pileata*										lC	3,5
Guira Tanager — *Hemithraupis guira*										R	1,2
Yellow-backed Tanager — *H. flavicollis*										U	1,2
Orange-headed Tanager — *Thlypopsis sordida*										U	3,5
Buff-bellied Tanager — *T. inornata*			cU								3,12
Rufous-chested Tanager — *T. ornata*					F		U	U			3,7,12
Brown-flanked Tanager — *T. pectoralis*							cU				3
Rust-and-Yellow Tanager — *T. ruficeps*							sU	sF			3
White-capped Tanager — *Sericossypha albocristata*							lU	lU			7
Common Bush-Tanager — *Chlorospingus ophthalmicus*								C			3,7
Yellow-throated Bush-Tanager — *C. flavigularis*									C		3
Short-billed Bush-Tanager — *C. parvirostris*								lC			3,7
Ash-throated Bush-Tanager — *C. canigularis*					nF				lC		7
Gray-hooded Bush-Tanager — *Cnemoscopus rubrirostris*							F				7
Black-capped Hemispingus — *Hemispingus atropileus*							C				7,8
Orange-browed Hemispingus — *H. calophrys*							sF				7
Parodi's Hemispingus — *H. parodii*							s?				8
Superciliaried Hemispingus — *H. superciliaris*					C		C				7
Oleaginous Hemispingus — *H. frontalis*								U			7
Black-eared Hemispingus — *H. melanotis*					C			F			7
Rufous-browed Hemispingus — *H. rufosuperciliaris*							cR				8
Black-headed Hemispingus — *H. verticalis*							nC				7,8

	WEST						EAST				
	sea and shore	arid tropical	arid subtropical	arid temperate	humid subtropical and temperate	puna	humid temperate	humid subtropical	humid upper tropical	humid tropical	habitats
†Drab Hemispingus — *H. xanthophthalmus*							C				7,8
Three-striped Hemispingus — *H. trifasciatus*							U				7,8
Black-and-White Tanager — *Conothraupis speculigera*		R			R					cR	3,15
Grass-Green Tanager — *Chlorornis riefferii*							F				7
Red-billed Pied Tanager — *Lamprospiza melanoleuca*										R	1
Magpie Tanager — *Cissopis leveriana*									U	C	3,5,6
Black-faced Tanager — *Schistochlamys melanopis*								U	U	/F	3,4
PLUSH-CAPPED FINCHES — Catamblyrhynchidae Plush-capped Finch — *Catamblyrhynchus diadema*					U		F	U			7,8
FINCHES — Fringillidae Buff-throated Saltator — *Saltator maximus*		nU							U	C	1,2
Grayish Saltator — *S. coerulescens*									C		3,5,6
Golden-billed Saltator — *S. aurantiirostris*			U	C							12
†Black-cowled Saltator — *S. nigriceps*					nU						3,7
Masked Saltator — *S. cinctus*							R	R			7,8
Streaked Saltator — *S. albicollis*		C	U								15,16,17
Yellow-shouldered Grosbeak — *Caryothraustes humeralis*										R	1,2,7
Slate-colored Grosbeak — *Pitylus grossus*									U	F	1,2
Red-capped Cardinal — *Paroaria gularis*										C	6
Yellow Grosbeak — *Pheucticus chrysopeplus* Golden-bellied Grosbeak — *P. chrysogaster*		U	F	U	U		R	R			3,15,16
Black-backed Grosbeak — *P. aureoventris*							U	U	?	R	3,7
Rose-breasted Grosbeak — *P. ludovicianus*										mR	3
Blue-Black Grosbeak — *Cyanocompsa cyanoides*		nU								U	1,2
Blue-Black Grassquit — *Volatinia jacarina*		U	C							U	3,16,17
Cinereous Finch — *Piezorhina cinerea*		C									14
*Slate-colored Seedeater — *Sporophila schistacea*									/U	/U	2,7
Plumbeous Seedeater — *S. plumbea*										sR	4
Variable Seedeater — *S. americana*		C								/C	3,5
Lined Seedeater — *S. lineola*										/C	3,5
Black-and-White Seedeater — *S. luctuosa*			/C	/C	/C			/C	U	R	3,12,17
Yellow-bellied Seedeater — *S. nigricollis*			/C	/C	/C			/C	?	?	3,12,17
Dull-colored Seedeater — *S. obscura*			U							U	3

77

		WEST				EAST					
	sea and shore	arid tropical	arid subtropical	arid temperate	humid subtropical and temperate	puna	humid temperate	humid subtropical	humid upper tropical	humid tropical	habitats
Double-collared Seedeater — *S. caerulescens*										mC	3,5,6
Parrot-billed Seedeater — *S. peruviana*		C	U								14,16,17
Drab Seedeater — *S. simplex*			U								16,17
Chestnut-bellied Seedeater — *S. castaneiventris*										C	3,5,6
Chestnut-throated Seedeater — *S. telasco*		F	C								14,16,17
Large-billed Seed-Finch — *Oryzoborus crassirostris*										lR	6
Greater Large-billed Seed-Finch — *O. maximiliani*										lR	6
Lesser (Thick-billed) Seed-Finch — *O. angolensis*								U	U	F	3,6
Band-tailed Seedeater — *Catamenia analis*			F	C							12
Plain-colored Seedeater — *C. inornata*				F			R				12
Paramo Seedeater — *C. homochroa*				R			R				8,9
Sulphur-throated Finch — *Gnathospiza taczanowskii*		lC									14
Stripe-tailed Yellow-Finch — *Sicalis citrina*							?	?			?
Puna Yellow-Finch — *S. lutea*						sC					10,12
Bright-rumped Yellow-Finch — *S. uropygialis*						C					10
Greenish Yellow-Finch — *S. olivascens*				lC							12,17
Orange-fronted Yellow-Finch — *S. columbiana*										?	5
Saffron Finch — *S. flaveola*		F									14,17
Grassland Yellow-Finch — *S. luteola*	U		U	U							17,20
Raimondi's Yellow-Finch — *S. raimondii*			lC								12,19
White-winged Diuca-Finch — *Diuca speculifera*						lC					12
Short-tailed Finch — *Idiopsar brachyurus*						sR					12
Gray-hooded Sierra-Finch — *Phrygilus gayi*				C		U					12
Black-hooded Sierra-Finch — *P. atriceps*				sC							12
Mourning Sierra-Finch — *P. fruticeti*				C							12
Plumbeous Sierra-Finch — *P. unicolor*					U	F	U				9,10
White-throated Sierra-Finch — *P. erythronotus*						sU					10
Ash-breasted Sierra-Finch — *P. plebejus*		lC	U	C		C					10,12, 14
Band-tailed Sierra-Finch — *P. alaudinus*		?	F	U							12,17
Slaty Finch — *Haplospiza rustica*					lU			lU	lU		7,8
Red-crested Finch — *Coryphospingus cucullatus*		cC									14
Crimson Finch — *Rhodospingus cruentus*		U									15,16
Pale-naped Brush-Finch — *Atlapetes pallidinucha*							nC				8,9
Rufous-naped Brush-Finch — *A. rufinucha*							C	C	C		3,8,9
Tricolored Brush-Finch — *A. tricolor*								U			3,7
Rufous-eared Brush-Finch — *A. rufigenis*				lF			sF				3,12,13

	WEST						EAST				
	sea and shore	arid tropical	arid subtropical	arid temperate	humid subtropical and temperate	puna	humid temperate	humid subtropical	humid upper tropical	humid tropical	habitats
White-winged Brush-Finch — *A. leucopterus*		C						nU			3,7,15
Slaty Brush-Finch — *A. schistaceus*							F				3,7
Bay-crowned Brush-Finch — *A. seebohmi*		R	F	U							12
Rusty-bellied Brush-Finch — *A. nationi*			U	C							12,13
White-headed Brush-Finch — *A. albiceps*		C									15,16
Chestnut-capped Brush-Finch — *A. brunneinucha*							nU	F	U		7
Stripe-headed Brush-Finch — *A. torquatus*			cF	F			F	U			7,12
Olive Finch — *Lysurus castaneiceps*								/R			7
Pectoral Sparrow — *Arremon taciturnus*										U	2
Orange-billed Sparrow — *A. aurantiirostris*		nU								U	1
Black-capped Sparrow — *A. abeillei*		F									15,16
Grassland Sparrow — *Myospiza humeralis*										sC	4
Yellow-browed Sparrow — *M. aurifrons*								U	U	C	3,5
Tumbes Sparrow — *Rhynchospiza stolzmanni*		F									14,15
Gray-winged Inca-Finch — *Incaspiza ortizi*			cU								12
Great Inca-Finch — *I. pulchra*			U								12
Rufous-backed Inca-Finch — *I. personata*				cU							12
Buff-bridled Inca-Finch — *I. laeta*			cF								14,15
Little Inca-Finch — *I. watkinsi*		cU									14
Rufous-collared Sparrow — *Zonotrichia capensis*	/F	/F	C	C	F	R	C	U	/U	/F	+
Wedge-tailed Grass-Finch — *Emberizoides herbicola*		c?								sC	4
Black-masked Finch — *Coryphaspiza melanotis*										sF	4
Slender-billed Finch — *Xenospingus concolor*			/F								16
Plain-tailed Warbling-Finch — *Poospiza alticola*				/U							12,13
Collared Warbling-Finch — *P. hispaniolensis*		U	U								14,15,16
Rufous-breasted Warbling-Finch — *P. rubecula*				/R							12
Chestnut-breasted Mountain-Finch — *Poospizopsis caesar*				sU							12
Thick-billed Siskin — *Carduelis [Spinus] crassirostris*				/C							12,13
Hooded Siskin — *C. [Spinus] magellanica*		U	C	C	F		U	U			+
Olivaceous Siskin — *C. [Spinus] olivacea*								U	U		3,7
Yellow-bellied Siskin — *C. [Spinus] xanthogastra*								sU			3
Black Siskin — *C. [Spinus] atrata*				/C		U					12,13
Yellow-rumped Siskin — *C. [Spinus] uropygialis*				R							14
Lesser Goldfinch — *C. [Spinus] psaltria*		/U	cU								3,15

Map 2. Principal highways and localities mentioned in the birdfinding section of this checklist.

BIRD FINDING IN PERU

Peru probably has more to offer the adventurous birder than any other country in the world. Unfortunately, many areas are nearly inaccessible due to transportation problems posed by the extraordinary topography. However, areas typical of the many habitats good for birding can be reached from some of the major highways. In the following pages we list some of the best and most accessible areas for good birding. For those adventurous spirits wishing to reach more inaccessible places, we suggest researching the type of habitat that would be of most interest and then planning an extended field visit, with the realization that accommodations are likely to be nonexistent.

In the brief discussion of birding in Peru that follows, we provide a general description of each area. Where additional references are available in the literature, particularly where there are papers that provide locality lists, we refer to them.

Lima and Paracas

Most international flights to Peru arrive in Lima. Birding in and around the city itself is not good, and we recommend travelling immediately to Paracas or north, especially if pressed for time. The parks and gardens of Lima attract a few species, but most of these can be seen in other parts of the country. Possibilities in the parks and residential areas of the city are White-winged Dove, Croaking Ground-Dove, Amazilia Hummingbird, Vermilion Flycatcher (a sooty-gray phase found only along the coast of Peru is common in the city), Southern Beardless Tyrannulet, Blue-and-White Swallow, Shiny Cowbird, Blue-Black Grassquit, Chestnut-throated Seedeater, Rufous-collared Sparrow, and Hooded Siskin. Many of the seabirds of Humboldt Current can be seen along Lima's shore. Particularly good are the beaches of Miraflores, Chorillos, and Villa. Boat trips can be arranged from the Port of Callao. Marshy areas near the city, such as those near the Villa Golf Club to the south, are good for Plumbeous Rail, Wren-like Rushbird, Many-colored Rush-Tyrant, Yellowish Pipit, and Peruvian Red-breasted Meadowlark.

Paracas Peninsula is a national park 250 kilometers south of Lima just west of the Panameri-can Highway. There are accommodations available at the comfortable Hotel Paracas or the less expensive Hosteria next door. Camping is also allowed, with permission secured from park headquarters. The extensive mudflats along the south shore of Paracas Bay and the rocky outer coasts of the peninsula teem with shorebirds (September to May) and seabirds. A tourist boat, for which reservations are required, leaves the Hotel Paracas daily and gives birders an opportunity to see the great colonies of boobies, pelicans, and cormorants on the Ballestas Islands, as well as a chance to see pelagic seabirds, such as shearwaters and petrels. South American Sea Lions are quite common on the islands, and Southern Fur Seals may also be seen. Birds of particular interest in the bay itself include Great Grebe, Chilean Flamingo, White-cheeked Pintail, Gray Gull, Band-tailed Gull, Kelp Gull, Inca Tern, Peruvian Tern, South American Tern, and a variety of North American shorebirds. During the winter (May to August) Puna Plover, Andean Lapwing, and Rufous-chested Dotterel are possibilities. Birds of the outer coast include Humboldt Penguin, Peruvian Diving-Petrel, Peruvian Pelican, Peruvian Booby, Guanay, Red-legged Cormorant, Andean Condor, Blackish Oystercatcher, and Seaside Cinclodes. Pelagic birds include Sooty Shearwater, Southern Fulmar, Cape Petrel, White-vented Storm-Petrel, Wilson's Storm-Petrel, Chilean Skua, and Swallow-tailed Gull. Landbirds are not numerous and can be seen with little effort, particularly along dry watercourses or in hedgerows near irrigated fields. In the latter habitats are Peruvian Thick-knee, Short-tailed Field-Tyrant, Peruvian Red-breasted Meadowlark, Drab Seedeater, Chestnut-throated Seedeater, and Slender-billed Finch.

Additional references for these areas include Parker and O'Neill (1976a), Koepcke (1970), and O'Neill and Plenge (MS).

Cordillera Blanca

All travelers to Peru should see this spectacular mountain range, and now the region is quite accessible. There are excellent accommodations in Huaráz and the other large towns of the Callejón de Huaylas. There is something for everyone here; it is a paradise for hikers, mountain climbers, and fishermen, and even those who have difficulty walking at high elevations can visit a *Polylepis* woodland, observe the high Andean flora and fauna, and enjoy the magnificent snow-covered peaks. For those who have only a few days to spend here we recommend two areas, both easy to reach. The recently-paved Pativilca-Huaráz road passes close to the shore of Lake Conococha (4100 m) in the uppermost part of the valley. In a few hours here even the most casual observer will become acquainted with the bird and plant life of the puna, including marsh and water birds like Puna Ibis, Andean Goose, Crested Duck, Speckled Teal, Yellow-billed Pintail, Giant Coot, and Andean Lapwing, and land birds such as Mountain Caracara and various miners, ground-tyrants, and yellow-finches. *The Birds of the Department of Lima* (Koepcke 1970) covers all the species that occur in the region, with the exception of a few woodland birds. Though hiking trails lead up into many quebradas throughout the mountain range, the easiest way to visit the shrub zone and *Polylepis* woodlands that occur on the upper mountain slopes at 3000 to 4200 m (10,000 to 14,000 ft) is to drive or be driven to Quebrada Llanganuco, above Yungay. The scenery is fantastic, and the *Polylepis* groves around the lakes at the upper end of the valley are among the most accessible in all of Peru. Here in a short time one can see quite a variety of birds, including Giant Conebill, Tit-like Dacnis, and possibly even the unusual White-cheeked Cotinga. Other special birds include Rusty-crowned Tit-Spinetail, Line-cheeked Spinetail, Stripe-headed Antpitta, Rufous-webbed Tyrant, Pied-crested Tit-Tyrant, Rufous-cheeked Brush-Finch, and hummingbirds such as Shining Sunbeam and Black Metaltail. The best woods are between the checkpoint at 3500 m (11,000 ft) and the lakes at 4000 m (12,500 ft), but *Polylepis* trees and *Gynoxys* shrubs, which are especially attractive to the Tit-like Dacnis, grow to above 4300 m (14,000 ft). Rarities like the Tawny Tit-Spinetail and Ash-breasted Tit-Tyrant may be found in the uppermost vegetation. There is regular taxi service from Yungay to Llanganuco.

For those who rent a car in Lima and drive to Huaráz we should mention a few additional localities along the way. Least Seedsnipe can often be seen flying up from the edge of the Panamerican Highway near Km 100 north of Lima and there is a nice coastal lagoon south of Huacho at "El Paraíso", several kilometers west of the road and just inside the beach. The shrub-cactus zone at 1500 to 2100 m (5000 to 7000 ft) of the mountains along the Pativilca-Conococha stretch is probably inhabited by the elusive Great Inca-Finch, although we haven't looked for it there.

The Central Highway: Lake Junín, Huánuco, Carpish, and Tingo María

The Central Highway of Peru is undoubtedly one of the engineering wonders of the world. The highway is the major link between Lima and the inland Amazonian forests, and provides a truly spectacular traveling experience. Although it is possible to drive nonstop from Lima to Huánuco in about ten hours via rented car or rented private taxi with driver, the serious birder should devote at least three days to this 435 kilometer stretch. The first day should be spent between Lima and San Mateo, a relatively short and easy trip that will serve as an introduction to Andean birds. The second day would best be reserved for the Casapalca-Chinchan-Marcapomacocha loop. Each of these two trips can be done round-trip from Lima quite easily. On the third day one should drive directly to Lake Junín and on to Huánuco.

Please keep in mind that kilometer markers often change as the road is surveyed for various purposes. In our discussion we try to avoid using kilometer markers in giving directions, but occasionally we must. Remember that those we list will not necessarily remain accurate.

Lima to Huánuco. From Lima eastward to Chosica the highway passes irrigated agricultural lands with many hedgerows; stopping is not advised along this section due to the heavy traffic and the lack of interesting birds. Near Km 44 (markers posted from Lima) east of Chosica, just beyond a railroad crossing on the north side of the road, there are flower gardens that attract such hummingbirds as Amazilia Hummingbird, Oasis Hummingbird, and Peruvian Sheartail. In nearby riparian growth along the Rimac River there are the typical Lima species and also Eared Dove, Bare-faced Ground-Dove (on the rocky arid slope), White-tipped Dove, Groove-billed Ani, Chiguanco Thrush, Long-tailed Mockingbird, Scrub Blackbird, and Yellow Grosbeak. About 60 kilometers further, just before San Mateo at the gas station and restaurant, there are flowering agaves that attract Giant Hummingbirds. Occasionally Andean Condor and Andean Swift are found overhead. Behind and to the right of the restaurant a trail leads down to the river where White-capped Dipper may be found. In the dense shrubbery are Black Metaltail, Sparkling Violetear, Cinereous Conebill, Black-throated and Slaty Flower-piercer, Blue-and-Yellow Tanager, and Rusty-bellied Brush-Finch. While continuing on from this stop into the town of San Mateo, watch for a narrow road that turns off to the right. It crosses a small bridge and railroad tracks before winding into a shrub zone (3500 m) and ending at a mine. In this shrub habitat species characteristic of the Andean Arid Temperate Zone may be seen, such as Striated Earthcreeper, Canyon Canastero, Bar-winged Cinclodes, Rusty-crowned Tit-Spinetail, White-browed Chat-Tyrant, Yellow-billed Tit-Tyrant, and Ash-breasted, Mourning, and Gray-hooded Sierra-Finch.

Once again on the main highway, proceed to the Marcapomacocha turnoff, which is on the left a short distance past Casapalca. Along this side road one can see many high-elevation land and water birds typical of the Puna Zone. The altitude is extreme (4500 m) and care should be taken not to overexert oneself. Specialties here include Ornate and Puna Tinamou, Silvery Grebe (on deep lakes), Puna Ibis, Andean Goose, Speckled Teal, Mountain Caracara, Gray-breasted Seedsnipe, Andean Lapwing, Diademed Sandpiper-Plover, Olivaceous Thornbill, Buff-breasted Earthcreeper, Streak-throated Canastero, Junin Canastero, ground-tyrants such as Ochre-naped, White-fronted, Rufous-naped, and Plain-capped, Bright-rumped Yellow-Finch, Gray-hooded and Plumbeous Sierra-Finch, and White-winged Diuca-Finch.

The high pass on the Central Highway is at Ticlio (4843 m), and the view of snowy peaks, glacier lakes, and mine tailing slopes of many colors is breathtaking. There is little need to stop from here until after passing through La Oroya. After La Oroya, between Km 199 and the Tarma turnoff, watch along the stream paralleling the road for Torrent Duck, White-winged Cinclodes, Andean Swallow, and sierra-finches. Past the Tarma turnoff the road gradually ascends the Pampa de Junín, an expansive grassland that supports a high density of raptors such as Puna Hawk, Cinereous Harrier, Mountain Caracara, Aplomado Falcon, American Kestrel, and Short-eared Owl. In this area Common Miner and Bright-rumped Yellow-Finch are also conspicuous.

After passing through Junín city the highway borders the eastern shore of Lake Junín, passing through wet pastures that teem with birds. Several days could easily be spent here observing and photographing the rather tame resident species, but overnight accommodations between La Oroya and Huánuco are poor. In the vicinity of Lake Junín one should have no trouble seeing many of Peru's highland water and marsh birds. These include White-tufted Grebe, Black-faced and Puna Ibis, Andean Goose, Crested Duck, Speckled Teal, Yellow-billed Pintail, Puna Teal, Andean Ruddy Duck, Mountain Caracara, Plumbeous Rail, Common Gallinule, Slate-colored and American Coot, Andean Lapwing, Puna Snipe, Andean Gull, Wren-like Rushbird, Many-colored Rush-Tyrant, and Andean Rufous-backed Negrito.

Be sure to continue on the main highway and not take the Cerro de Pasco turnoff. Beyond the turnoff are several more lakes and ponds, including one large deep lake on the left side, good for Silvery Grebe and Giant Coot, and several shallow smaller ponds on the right, good for Crested Duck. As the descent to Huánuco begins, the first prominent vegetation below the puna grassland is *Polylepis* woodland (3700 m). Just above the village of La Quinua, the road drops into a beautiful park-like area of *Polylepis* trees, which look like gnarled olive trees with peeling reddish bark and tiny leaves. This unique habitat is one of the most distinctive of Andean environments. Some of the birds found here are Black-winged Ground-Dove, Band-winged Nightjar, Giant Hummingbird, Sparkling Violetear, Shining Sunbeam, Black Metaltail, Bar-winged Cinclodes, Andean Tit-Spinetail, Line-cheeked Spinetail, Stripe-headed Antpitta, Red-crested Cotinga, Black-billed Shrike-Tyrant, Rufous-webbed Tyrant, D'Orbigny's Chat-Tyrant, White-browed Chat-Tyrant, Tufted and Pied-crested Tit-Tyrant, Brown-bellied Swallow, House Wren, Chiguanco Thrush, Black-throated Flower-piercer, Blue-and-Yellow Tanager, Giant Conebill, Golden-billed Saltator, and Hooded and Black Siskin.

Between Huariaca and Huánuco city the descent is rapid. Scan the sky for Black-chested Buzzard-Eagle and Red-backed Hawk, which soar high over the valley. Stopping along this stretch is difficult and generally unprofitable, although Brown-flanked Tanager may be seen in dense thickets along the stream between 2000 to 3000 m. This is the only local endemic that doesn't range as high as the *Polylepis* woodlands.

Huánuco and Carpish Pass. There are good accommodations in Huánuco; we recommend the Hotel de Turistas. The region around the city is quite arid, with cacti and agave prominent on the slopes. Hedgerows and washes lined with pepper-trees border irrigated farmlands on the valley floor. Some species one should encounter near town are Eared Dove, Croaking and Plain-breasted Ground-Dove, White-bellied Hummingbird, Fasciated Wren, Peruvian Red-breasted Meadowlark, and Black-and-White Seedeater. In the irrigated areas are Smooth-billed Ani, Tropical Kingbird, and Blue-Gray and Black-bellied Tanager.

One should plan on staying in Huánuco for several days in order to work the Carpish Pass region. In the vicinity of the pass is the most accessible cloud forest in Peru. Just one hour by taxi northeast of arid Huánuco the highway enters a humid, mist-shrouded forest of moss-and bromeliad-laden trees with dense stands of *Chusquea* bamboo. Leave Huánuco well before dawn and drive nonstop through the Carpish Tunnel and then down the east slope about eight kilometers, where a corrugated tin-roofed shed marks the beginning of the Paty Trail, which leads to a tea plantation several thousand feet below in the valley. It is best to pull well off the roadway into the grassy parking area next to the shed and talk to the guard living there. He will watch the car and point out the trailhead; don't forget to present him with a token of appreciation such as cigarettes or money.

The upper few hundred yards of the trail are steep, narrow and usually slippery. Early in the morning, especially on foggy days, this area abounds with flocks of tanagers, flower-piercers, ovenbirds, and other small passerines moving through the mossy forest. Along the upper part of the trail from 2300 to 2400 m (7500 to 8000 ft) characteristic birds of the Humid Temperate Zone are common. In addition to the flocks moving through the treetops are understory birds such as woodcreepers, ovenbirds, a few antbirds, and various cryptically-colored and solitary flycatchers, tinamous, quail-doves, and antpittas (see Parker and O'Neill 1976b for a complete list of birds of the Carpish region). Along the trail fruiting trees of the family Melastomataceae attract numbers of frugivores, such as trogons, fruiteaters, thrushes, and tanagers, especially mountain-tanagers and members of the genus *Tangara*.

After about a quarter of a mile the trail levels out and is bordered on the right by a large clearing. Here at the forest edge and a little farther along, where the trail passes through second-growth woodland with numerous *Cecropia* trees, are found representatives of the Humid Subtropical Zone. Watch particularly for flowering *Cecropia*, which attract such nectarivores as the Golden-collared Honeycreeper. A short distance below this level area one will come to the upper edge of the tea plantation at 2050 m (6800 ft). Only scattered patches of forest remain below this area. Higher up along the highway on both sides of the tunnel, one may walk for several kilometers.

It is possible to reach two more distinctive Andean habitats several thousand feet above the Carpish Tunnel. These are the treeline elfin forest and the páramo from 2900 to 3700 m (9500 to 12,000 ft). In recent years some of the rarest of Peruvian birds have been found in this region, including several species new to science. The treeline forest and páramo may be reached from Pachachupán. A fairly strenuous pack trip is involved. More specific directions are given by Parker and O'Neill (1976b).

Huánuco to Tingo María. Between Huánuco and Tingo María is the deep forested gorge of the Río Chinchavito, which is one of the best places in the country to see Andean Cock-of-the-Rock. Stop (between Km 491 and 494) in early morning if possible and walk slowly along the river gorge, scanning the forest canopy on the opposite side of the river. Other interesting birds in the vicinity are Fasciated Tiger-Heron, Golden-headed Quetzal, Amazonian Umbrellabird, Golden-crowned and Cliff Flycatcher, Torrent Tyrannulet, White-capped Dipper, and River Warbler. Just before dawn and at dusk Lyre-tailed Nightjar is occasionally seen on the roadway.

Tingo María and Vicinity. Most visitors to Tingo María stay at the comfortable Hotel de Turistas. A channel of the Río Huallaga passes within a few hundred yards of the hotel, and from the restaurant one has a lovely view of the mountains rising abruptly to the west. The hotel grounds provide some good birding, but the best area near the hotel is the Cueva de las Lechuzas (Oilbird Cave) in the Parque Nacional Tingo María, which is eight kilometers north of town. A narrow gravel road, closed to all but local traffic, leads several kilometers through second-growth forest from the park entrance to the cave and beyond. This road is good for Humid Tropical Zone birds, including local specialties such as Blue-headed Macaw and Black-bellied Tanager. The oilbird cave itself is spectacular. A good flashlight is necessary, as most of the oilbirds are on high ledges in the dim recesses of the cave. Warning signs are posted stating the presence of histoplasmosis, a dust-borne fungal disease, so take care not to stir the cave floor unnecessarily.

A major reason for visiting Tingo María is for access to the Cordillera (Divisoria) Azul, which lies between Tingo María and Pucallpa and forms the boundary between the departments of Huánuco and Ucayali (formerly Loreto). The cloud forests that cover the ridges of this range at altitudes of 1150 to 1500 m (3800 to 5000 ft) are rich in bird and plant life not easily observed elsewhere in Peru.

About 40 kilometers northeast of Tingo María the Central Highway rises into cloud forest. The first few kilometers above the tea plantations are in the Humid Upper Tropical Zone. Some of the characteristic birds of this tall, mossy forest are Spotted, Golden, and Golden-eared Tanager. In addition, Humid Tropical Zone species such as Paradise, Green-and-Gold, and Bay-headed Tanager reach their upper limit of distribution here. Higher up in Subtropical Zone forest one can find Blue-browed and Vermilion Tanager, and such special birds as Wattled Guan, Black-mandibled Toucan, and Crested and Golden-headed Quetzal.

Just about two kilometers beyond the Divisoria Pass (1580 m) is a trail leading off to the south. The trail provides an opportunity to walk through undisturbed forest of great beauty. This habitat is not easy to bird, and a tape recorder is necessary for luring out many of the more secretive species. For a complete list of birds found in the Cordillera Azul see Parker and O'Neill (1981).

Just before the Divisoria, in the foothills between the Aucayacu turnoff and the tea plantations, is another birding locality, Santa Elena. Several trails lead from the coffee plantation into forest. Some special birds of Santa Elena are Crested Foliage-gleaner, Stipple-throated Antwren, Rufous-tailed Antwren, Spot-winged Antbird, Sooty Antbird, White-plumed Antbird, Carmiol's Tanager, Yellow-crested Tanager, and Orange-billed Sparrow. For specific details and maps, refer to Parker and O'Neill (1981).

Continuing on the Central Highway toward Pucallpa, one soon encounters the spectacular Boquerón del Padre Abad, a deep canyon on the east side of the Cordillera Azul that cuts through forest-covered foothills. East of the Boquerón is level rainforest, stretching the remainder of the drive to Pucallpa. Pucallpa offers good birding around Lake Yarinacocha (see O'Neill and Pearson 1974). There are several nice tourist lodges, such as La Cabaña, but the area has been settled for many years and birds like trumpeters, guans, and macaws are long gone.

Nazca to Abancay and Cuzco

This is not a frequently travelled route, but there are several very interesting places along it. Only three hours east of Nazca is the Reserva Nacional de Pampa Galeras, the largest sanctuary for the vicuña, and a very beautiful place. The wide, rolling grasslands here are populated by thousands of these Andean camels, and they may be observed easily and photographed at close range. Puna Zone birds abound and *Polylepis* woodlands are within walking distance of the road and headquarter buildings (see Brokaw 1976). Unfortunately no accommodations are available on the reserve, but there are hotels in Puquio to the east, so one may spend a day driving the roads on the reserve, a night in Puquio, and the next day returning to Lima or Nazca. On the arid, rocky western slopes of the cordillera below the reserve to the west at 2500 to 3400 m (8000 to 11,000 ft) watch for Thick-billed Miner, Cactus Canastero, and Raimondi's Yellow-Finch.

Those who continue east from Puquio towards Abancay and Cuzco should, if possible, stop at the large lakes near the roadway in the high puna between Puquio and Chalhuanca. Giant Coots, Chilean Flamingos, and thousands of ducks can be seen on these lakes, and views of the Quechua herders with their sheep, llamas, alpacas, and even attendant vicuñas are alone worth the journey. Leaving the high grassland, the road eventually drops into the upper Apurimac River valley, and in doing so passes through *Polylepis* scrub (the first tree growth below the grassland) and shrubbery about 29 kilometers west of Chalhuanca, where we have seen Spot-winged Pigeon, Bearded Mountaineer, Creamy-crested Spinetail, Rusty-fronted Canastero, Tit-like Dacnis, and Chestnut-breasted Mountain-Finch.

Those who decide to spend a day or two in Abancay can hike into the Humid Temperate Zone forest on the slopes above the town to the north. This is the only known locality for Coursen's Spinetail, a species described to science only recently. Many other cloud forest birds occur here, and there is dry tropical forest lower down along the Apurimac River where different birds are to be observed, such as White-eared Puffbird and White-winged Black-Tyrant.

Cuzco

Nearly everyone who visits Peru will spend at least a few days in Cuzco. Rental cars are available in the city, though most of the following birding localities can be reached easily by other means, including buses and taxis.

The closest place to see a variety of water, marsh, and montane scrub birds is the Huaparcay

Lakes area 25 kilometers south of the city along the road to Puno. Just beyond Km 24 (road markers measured from the Cuzco city limits) two dirt roads on the right lead to the marsh edge. The second of these passes a row of houses and continues to a club of some sort; a large lake is on the right and hills covered with shrubs, low trees, and cacti are on the left. One of the most unusual birds of the area is the Bearded Mountaineer, a large showy hummingbird that frequents tree tobacco growing in ravines, especially at a point where an old dirt road turns off to the left and winds up to the main highway. In a few hours around the lake up to 60 species can be observed, among them White-tufted Grebe, Silvery Grebe, Puna Ibis, Speckled Teal, Yellow-billed Pintail, Puna Teal, Cinereous Harrier, Aplomado Falcon, Plumbeous Rail, Andean Lapwing, Andean Gull, Bare-faced Ground-Dove, Sparkling Violetear, Giant Hummingbird, Slender-billed Miner, Wren-like Rushbird, Rusty-fronted Canastero, Rufous-naped, White-browed, Puna, and Spot-billed Ground-Tyrant, Andean Rufous-backed Negrito, White-browed Chat-Tyrant, Yellow-billed Tit-Tyrant, Chiguanco Thrush, Yellow-winged Blackbird, Blue-and-Yellow Tanager, Band-tailed Seedeater, Greenish Yellow-Finch, Mourning and Ash-breasted Sierra-Finch, and Rufous-collared Sparrow.

The train to Macchu Picchu passes through beautiful agricultural lands north of the city, where Mountain Caracaras and Andean Lapwings can be seen in the fields, and Red-backed Hawks and American Kestrels perch in the willows and alders along the edges. From Pachar station the tracks parallel the Urubamba River, and Speckled Teal and Andean Gull are frequently visible on the water and shore. Downstream from Ollantaytambo the Urubamba narrows and rushes over large smooth boulders; on these the careful observer will see Torrent Duck and White-capped Dipper. Both of these can also be seen along the river above and below the train station at Macchu Picchu, where Fasciated Tiger-Heron and Torrent Tyrannulet can also be found.

The area around the Macchu Picchu ruins is not very good for birds. Only shrubbery and scattered thickets of short trees and bamboo remain. Some of the birds to be expected are Black-tailed Trainbearer, White-winged Black-Tyrant, Tufted Tit-Tyrant, White-crested and Sierran Elaenia, Blue-and-White Swallow, Chiguanco Thrush, Spectacled Redstart, Cinereous Conebill, Slaty and Black-throated Flower-piercer, Blue-capped Tanager, Blue-and-Yellow Tanager, Rust-and-Yellow Tanager, Streak-necked Flycatcher, Rufous-collared Sparrow, and Rufous-capped Brush-Finch. A soon-to-be-described *Thryothorus* wren (rust-colored above with black and white streaked underparts) is fairly common in bamboo thickets.

The best birding at Macchu Picchu is along the river from the train station downstream. Those who visit the ruins for just one day will arrive late in the morning, and there is usually time later in the afternoon to walk down the tracks and observe birds and plants. For a list of the bird possibilities see the lists for Carpish (Parker and O'Neill 1976b). Andean Cock-of-the-Rock is frequently seen flying through the trees where the tracks bend sharply to the right, a few hundred yards below the station.

For excellent birding and great views of the mountains, particularly of the peak and glacier named Veronica, the road from Ollantaytambo to Quillabamba is unsurpassed in the entire Cuzco region. Many of the south Peruvian endemics can be seen along this road. Until recently there was bus service to Quillabamba, but we have heard that this has been discontinued. There is, however, regular truck traffic, and the road is good enough for just about any kind of vehicle. At least two days should be set aside to cover all of the habitats along this road. From overnight accommodations in Urubamba or Ollantaytambo, where rooms should be reserved long in advance, a very early start is required to reach the cloud forest north of the pass at Abra Malaga before mid-morning. It takes about two hours to reach elfin treeline forest. There is continuous cloud forest from timberline at 3500 m (11,500 ft) down to San Luis, a restaurant-truck stop at 2700 m (9000 ft). Few roads in Peru pass through high forest and grassland of this kind, and many special birds can be observed. Some of these are Great Sapphirewing, Violet-throated

Star-frontlet, Sapphire-vented Puffleg, Scaled Metaltail, Tyrian Metaltail, Marcapata Spinetail, Puna Thistletail, Pearled Treerunner, Streaked Tuftedcheek, Undulated Antpitta, Andean Tapaculo, Red-crested Cotinga, Brown-backed Chat-Tyrant, White-throated Tyrannulet, Ochraceous-breasted Flycatcher, Unstreaked Tit-Tyrant, Pale-footed Swallow, White-browed Conebill, Blue-backed Conebill, Glossy Flower-piercer, Masked Flower-piercer, Tit-like Dacnis, Scarlet-bellied Mountain-Tanager, Buff-breasted Mountain-Tanager, Chestnut-bellied Mountain-Tanager, Hooded Mountain-Tanager, Three-striped Hemispingus, Citrine Warbler, and Slaty Brush-Finch (see also Parker and O'Neill 1980). In the grassland on either side of Abra Malaga puna birds such as Black-faced Ibis (along streams), Andean Goose, Gray-breasted Seedsnipe, Streak-throated Canastero, Bright-rumped Yellow-Finch, White-winged Diuca-Finch, and Plumbeous Sierra-Finch may be found, and in small *Polylepis* groves a few kilometers south of the pass on the east side of the road rarities like White-browed and Tawny Tit-Spinetail, Line-fronted Canastero, Ash-breasted Tit-Tyrant, and Giant Conebill have been observed.

The shrub zone about one hour above Ollantaytambo around the Peñas ruins is also very good. The best habitat is between the ruins and the grassland higher up. This locality can be covered in a few hours. Look for Andean Condor and Andean Swift high up over the cliffs, and Shining Sunbeam, White-tufted Sunbeam, Creamy-crested Spinetail, Rusty-fronted Canastero, Brown-bellied Swallow, Black-throated Flower-piercer, Tit-like Dacnis, Golden-billed Saltator, Gray-hooded Sierra-Finch, Chestnut-breasted Mountain-Finch, and Hooded Siskin in shrubbery and trees.

Highway from Cuzco to Marcapata, Quincemil, and Puerto Maldonado

This route is very productive, as it traverses nearly all the Andean and lowland tropical habitats, but transportation is limited to trucks or sturdy rented vehicles. During the rainy season from November to April stretches of the road may be impassable, especially in the lowlands. Most interesting is the cloud forest just below the village of Marcapata at 2700 m (9000 ft), where many of the Abra Malaga forest birds can be seen. Also of interest is the hill forest east of Quincemil, and the lowland rainforest that borders much of the road from Santa Rosa to Puerto Maldonado. Several years ago the best forest was near Km 106 west of Puerto Maldonado, and there were clearings for camping there. The entire journey from Cuzco to Puerto Maldonado takes about three days, while the daily jet flight takes one-half hour.

Puerto Maldonado is a rapidly growing frontier town surrounded by vast forests. Several good tourist lodges may be reached by boat from town. One of the main differences between this region and Iquitos and Pucallpa is in the degree to which man has persecuted the larger forest animals. For example, large birds like guans and macaws are nearly extinct in the vicinity of these latter two towns, while they survive in the vicinity of Puerto Maldonado. More than five hundred species of birds and a variety of mammals have been recorded at Explorer's Inn, about 60 kilometers up the Río Tambopata from Puerto Maldonado.

Explorer's Inn is in a completely unpopulated area and is surrounded by a government forest reserve of 5600 hectares. The great variety of Humid Tropical Zone micro-habitats on the reserve is partly responsible for the amazing avian diversity, which is the highest for any single locality in the world. Good trails traverse all habitat types, and dugout canoes are available for birding the oxbow lakes and the river. The best time to visit the region is between May and October. From October to April the daily jet flights may be interrupted by rain, although the birds are quite active and most nesting is taking place. At the present time the owners of Explorer's Inn offer a special daily rate to birders, which includes round-trip canoe transportation from Puerto Maldonado to the Inn, three meals, and lodging. This only applies to stays of six days or more. For more information on the special rate, and for bird and mammal lists, write

Peruvian Safaris, Garcilazo de la Vega 1334, Lima, Peru. For a brief discussion of the ecology of the area and a list of some of the more interesting birds see Parker (1980).

Puno

Lake Titicaca is quite beautiful, but its birds, with the exception of one, can be found easily in many other places in the Andes. The endemic Short-winged Grebe is not difficult to find along the west shore of the lake, where the road to Desaguadero passes quite close to the shore. Boats can be hired there for those who wish to get close to the grebes and other birds. The tourist boats to Uros Island are also worth taking.

Arequipa

From this immaculate city most naturalists will want to visit the upper slopes of Mt. Picchu-picchu on the road to Puno, and the puna grasslands and lakes higher up. Above Chiguata the road passes through a shrub zone and *Polylepis* scrub; from 3000 to 3700 m (10,000 to 12,000 ft) several stops should be made to look for such specialties as White-throated Earthcreeper, Straight-billed Earthcreeper, Creamy-breasted Canastero, D'Orbigny's Chat-Tyrant, Giant Conebill, Black-hooded Sierra-Finch, and Black Siskin. This is also one of the few known localities for Tamarugo Conebill, a bird described to science in 1968, which looks like a Cinereous Conebill but has rufous around the eyes and on the throat and upper breast. The road continues up into the puna and passes along the north shore of Lake Salinas, where there are usually thousands of flamingos (Chilean, James', and Andean in order of decreasing abundance), Puna Plover, Andean Avocet, and Gray-breasted Seedsnipe. On the slopes of the ridge north of the lake we have observed Puna and Ornate Tinamou, Rufous-bellied Seedsnipe, and White-throated Sierra-Finch. Golden-spotted Ground-Dove can be seen to the northeast of the lake, generally not far from human habitations. Vicuñas are becoming more common throughout the area, especially in the grassland on the north side of the road between the lake and the *Polylepis* scrub zone to the west.

Coastal ponds and marshes south of Mollendo and Mejia are quite good for waders, ducks, and shorebirds (see Hughes 1970).

Tumbes

Tumbes is good for desert scrub birding, especially to the north and along the road to Puerto Pizarro, where boat trips into the mangroves can be arranged. Several roads to the east lead to dry tropical forest. Masked Water-Tyrant can be seen along the Tumbes River near town. Common desert birds of northwest Peru include endemics (also found in southwest Ecuador) such as Pacific Parrotlet, Amazilia Hummingbird, Scarlet-backed Woodpecker, Necklaced Spinetail, Collared Antshrike, Baird's and Rufous Flycatcher (local), Fasciated Wren, Superciliated Wren, Long-tailed Mockingbird, White-edged Oriole, and Cinereous Finch.

Piura

The most interesting area near Piura is the road to Huancabamba. Buses leave almost daily for this highland town; the road traverses a variety of habitats and crosses the Western Cordillera above Canchaque. At upper elevations of 2500 to 3000 m (8000 to 10,000 ft) it passes through humid temperate forest and *Polylepis* woodland. A trail leads from the pass down about 1200 m into the valley of Canchaque through forest, but much of this habitat is now being destroyed. Many interesting birds can be seen here, including Bearded Guan, Rainbow Starfrontlet, Purple-throated Sunangel, Golden-headed Quetzal, Line-cheeked Spinetail, Gray-headed Antbird, Unicolored Tapaculo, Turquoise Jay, and Three-banded Warbler. Lower on the west side, above Canchaque near "Puente Fierro," other specialties like Black-hooded Saltator and Chapman's Antshrike may be seen in roadside scrub.

The Huancacamba Valley is dry and heavily cultivated. A poor dirt road leads from town to the village of Sapalache to the northeast. A few kilometers east of town this road passes through a small area of desert scrub at 2100 m (7000 ft) where the rare Gray-winged Inca-Finch has been found, as well as Spot-throated Hummingbird, Purple-collared Woodstar, Black-necked Wood-pecker, Tawny-crowned Pygmy-Tyrant, Yellow-billed Tit-Tyrant, and Ash-breasted Sierra-Finch.

For the adventuresome, there is a trail that crosses the mountains to the east of Sapalache; it branches off from the Huancabamba-Sapalache road just east of the village of Shapaya and winds up through farmland into cloud forest from 2500 m (8000 ft) upwards, eventually reaching elfin forest and paramo vegetation at 3000 m (10,000 ft). The ridge is known as Cerro Chinguela, and from the pass the trail rapidly descends through beautiful cloud forest. In the upper forest and páramo researchers have recently found many species previously unrecorded in Peru, and one species new to science, the Neblina Metaltail (Graves 1980). Other birds of interest are Andean and Banded Snipe, Bearded Guan, Rusty-faced Parrot, Buff-winged Star-frontlet, Tourmaline Sunangel, Glowing Puffleg, Rainbow-bearded Thornbill, Mouse-brown Thistletail, Chestnut-naped Antpitta, Slate-crowned Antpitta, Peruvian Antpitta (lower on east slope at 2250 m), Ash-colored Tapaculo, Ocellated Tapaculo, Orange-banded Flycatcher, Pale-footed Swallow, Rufous Wren, Plain-tailed Wren, Black-chested and Masked Mountain-Tanager, Golden-crowned Tanager, Black-headed Hemispingus, and Pale-naped Brush-Finch. Many of these birds can be easily observed in Colombia and Ecuador, but few areas in those countries match the beauty of the region east of Huancabamba. It takes about 6 hours to hike from Shapaya to the pass on Cerro Chinguela, where one can camp at the forest edge. Guides and pack animals can be found in Huancabamba or Shapaya. Be forewarned that it rains heavily through much of the year in the high forest and páramo. Eventually the Huancabamba-Tabaconas-Jaen road will be completed and many of the above birds will be within walking distance of a car or truck.

Accommodations are available in Canchaque and Huancabamba; the Piura-Huancabamba bus ride takes about 8 hours. This trip and the localities mentioned above are not recommended to those who are not used to travelling under arduous conditions.

Chiclayo

From this bustling northwest Peruvian city one may travel by bus or car into the Marañón River valley and beyond. The following local trips may also be taken.

Driving south on the Panamerican Highway, watch for signs to Puerto Etén on the right; just north of this coastal village there are several marshes that attract numerous ducks, shorebirds, Wren-like Rushbird, Many-colored Rush-Tyrant, and Yellowish Pipit. In the desert along the Panamerican Highway a little farther south at Km 756 we've repeatedly observed Least Seed-snipe and Tawny-throated Dotterel. From the village of Mocupe, also on the main highway, the gravel road heading west to Laguna crosses an area of *Acacia* and *Capparis* trees about one-half kilometer north of the tiny village of Rafán; this is one of the few localities for Peruvian Plantcutter, and most of the birds mentioned in the Tumbes account are also here.

North of Chiclayo one has to drive to beyond Jayanca to get into good desert scrub habitat. The Chiclayo-Jayanca stretch is densely populated, though in the agricultural fields Savanna Hawk may be seen, and Pearl Kite is often on the telephone wires. Between Jayanca and Motupe and Olmos numerous stops can be made in the desert, and in areas of mesquite bordering streams and washes. East of Olmos the highway to the Marañón Valley winds up through dry tropical forest and remnant patches of cloud forest; a day along this road will produce many of the birds listed for the upper elevations of the Huancabamba road. We have stopped at a wooded ravine and stream on the right about 34 kilometers from Olmos for Henna-hooded Foliage-gleaner, Chapman's Antshrike, and Black-hooded Saltator. Other forest patches can be found higher upon the slopes about 12 kilometers farther on. The desert species listed for Tumbes can be observed throughout the lowlands east of Olmos.

Those who wish to visit the dry Marañón River valley and the jungle to the east should travel by car or bus from Chiclayo to Bagua Chica. To the north and west of this town, and along the road to Jaen, several of the Marañón endemics may be found in the scrub, including Marañón Crescentchest, Marañón Thrush, and Little Inca-Finch. Rufous-fronted Thornbird and Red-crested Finch are common here as well.

Another interesting route is the Bagua-Chachapoyas road. Even better is the very new Bagua-Pedro Ruíz-Rioja road, which crosses the eastern cordilleran cloud forest (Humid Upper Tropical and Humid Subtropical Zones) about 80 kilometers northwest of Rioja. The Long-whiskered Owlet was discovered along this road and the Marvelous Spatuletail may be observed above Pedro Ruíz (see Parker 1976). Unfortunately few or no accommodations are available between Pedro Ruíz and Rioja, but one can travel by bus or truck and camp along the way. For lists of cloud forest birds see Parker and O'Neill (1976a,b). There are also regular plane flights to Rioja from Chiclayo or Tarapoto.

It is also possible to travel by truck to Leimeibamba-Balsas-Celendin-Cajamarca, but this is a rough, dusty trip. The main purpose for making this journey would be to see the spectacular Marañón valley and to search for some of its most interesting endemic birds. From Leimeibamba the narrow road gradually ascends to a pass, where high cloud forest remains, and then crosses to the west into the Marañón drainage. Between 2100 and 2500 m (7000 and 8000 ft) the Great Spinetail can be found in dense shrubbery on the steep slopes, and lower down in the open, dry forest above Balsas the beautiful Buff-bridled Inca-Finch may be seen. Peruvian Pigeons should be looked for in trees along the river near Balsas. The best single locality for birds of the throrn scrub is "Hacienda Limon," a small agricultural area on the west slope of the valley, west of Balsas. In the *Acacia* woods and in bushes on the slopes above the farmland, some local and rare birds may be found. Most notable among these are Chestnut-backed Thornbird and Gray-winged Inca-Finch. Also look for Line-cheeked Spinetail, Chestnut-crowned Antpitta, Spot-throated Hummingbird, Marañón Thrush, and White-winged Black-Tyrant. Yellow-faced Parrotlets are also common in the Balsas region.

Cajamarca is not to be recommended to those searching for natural areas; the region is densely settled and little original vegetation has survived. There are, however, several nice hotels there, and it is a good overnight stop for those travelling from Trujillo to Balsas, the alternative way of reaching the Marañón valley and perhaps the easiest.

From Bagua Chica travellers may also visit the humid rainforests of the foothill country east of the Andes. The road to Aramongo and Chiriaco crosses forested hills that are rapidly being cleared, but east of the latter village much forest remains. This is Aguaruna Indian territory. Eventually the road east of Chiriaco is to be extended well out into lowland forest, and this will no doubt be an excellent region for birding. The narrow and usually muddy road from the military base at Mesones Muro to the river post at Urakusa crosses several low ranges of hills that reach about 600 m in elevation. In the epiphyte-laden forests near the crests of the ridges the Orange-throated Tanager (*Wetmorethraupis sterrhopteron*) has been seen. This is the only accessible locality for this recently-discovered Peruvian endemic (see Lowery and O'Neill 1964).

LITERATURE CITED

American Ornithologists' Union. 1957. Check-list of North American Birds, 5th edition. Baltimore: American Ornithologists' Union. 691 pp.

———. 1973. Thirty-second supplement to the American Ornithologists' Union Check-list of North American Birds. Auk 90:411–419.

———. 1976. Thirty-third supplement to the American Ornithologists' Union Check-list of North American Birds. Auk 93:875–879.

Blake, E. R. 1971. A new species of spinetail (*Synallaxis*) from Peru. Auk 88:179.

———. 1977. Manual of Neotropical Birds, Vol. 1. Spheniscidae (Penguins) to Laridae (Gulls and Allies). Chicago: University of Chicago Press. 674 pp.

Blake, E. R., and P. Hocking. 1974. Two new species of tanager from Peru. Wilson Bulletin 86:321–324.

Brokaw, H. P. 1976. Birds of Pampa Galeras, Peru. Delmarva Ornithologist 11:26–30.

Butler, T. Y. 1979. The Birds of Ecuador and the Galapagos Archipelago. Portsmouth, New Hampshire: The Ramphastos Agency. xviii + 68 pp.

Chapman, F. M. 1921. Descriptions of proposed new birds from Colombia, Ecuador, Peru, and Brazil. American Museum of Natural History Novitates 18:1–12.

———. 1926. The distribution of bird-life in Ecuador: a contribution to the study of the origin of Andean bird-life. American Museum of Natural History Bulletin 55:1–784.

Delacour, J., and D. Amadon. 1973. Curassows and Related Birds. New York: American Museum of Natural History. 274 pp.

Donahue, P., T. A. Parker, III, and B. Sorrie. MS. The Birds of the Tambopata Reserve.

Fitzpatrick, J. W., and J. P. O'Neill. 1979. A new tody-tyrant from northern Peru. Auk 96:443–447.

Fitzpatrick, J. W., J. W. Terborgh, and D. E. Willard. 1977. A new species of wood-wren from Peru. Auk 94:195–201.

Fitzpatrick, J. W., D. E. Willard, and J. W. Terborgh. 1979. A new species of hummingbird from Peru. Wilson Bulletin 91:177–186.

Goodall, J. D., A. W. Johnson, and R. A. Philippi. 1946 and 1951. Las Aves de Chile, su Conocimiento y sus Costumbres. 2 Vols. Buenos Aires: Platt Establecimientos Gráficos S. A. 358 pp. and 445 pp.

———. 1957 and 1964. Las Aves de Chile, su Conocimiento y sus Costumbres. 2 Suppl. Buenos Aires: Platt Establecimientos Gráficos S. A.

Graham, G. L., G. R. Graves, T. S. Schulenberg, and J. P. O'Neill. 1980. Seventeen bird species new to Peru from the Pampas de Heath. Auk 97:366-370.

Graves, G. R. 1980. A new species of metaltail hummingbird from northern Peru. Wilson Bulletin 92:1–7.

———. (in press). Speciation in the Carbonated Flower-piercer (*Diglossa carbonaria*) complex of the Andes. Condor.

Haffer, J. 1974. Avian Speciation in Tropical South America with a Systematic Survey of the Toucans (Ramphastidae) and Jacamars (Galbulidae). Cambridge, Massachusetts: Nuttall Ornithological Club, Publication 14. 390 pp.

Hilty, S. L., and W. L. Brown. MS. A Guide to the Birds of Colombia. (forthcoming from Princeton University Press, Princeton, New Jersey).

Hughes, R. A. 1970. Notes on the birds of the Mollendo district, southwest Peru. Ibis 112:229–241.

Johnson, A. W. 1965 and 1967. The Birds of Chile and Adjacent Regions of Argentina, Bolivia and Peru. 2 Vols. Buenos Aires: Platt Establecimientos Gráficos S. A. 398 pp. and 446 pp.

———. 1972. Supplement to the Birds of Chile and Adjacent Regions of Argentina, Bolivia and Peru. Buenos Aires: Platt Establecimientos Gráficos S. A. 116 pp.

Johnson, A. W., and W. R. Millie. 1972. A new species of conebill (*Conirostrum*) from northern Chile. *In* A. W. Johnson, ed., Supplement to the Birds of Chile and Adjacent Regions of Argentina, Bolivia, and Peru, pp. 6–8. Buenos Aires: Platt Establecimientos Gráficos S. A.

Koepcke, M. 1964. Las Aves del Departamento de Lima. Lima: Gráfica Morsom. 128 pp.

———. 1970. The Birds of the Department of Lima, Peru. Wynnewood, Pennsylvania: Livingston Publishing Company. 144 pp.

Lowery, G. H., Jr., and J. P. O'Neill. 1964. A new genus and species of tanager from Peru. Auk 81:125–131.

Lowery, G. H., Jr., and D. A. Tallman. 1976. A new genus and species of nine-primaried oscine of uncertain affinities from Peru. Auk 93:415–428.

Meyer de Schauensee, R. 1966. The Species of Birds of South America with Their Distribution. Narberth, Pennsylvania: Livingston Publishing Company. 577 pp.

———. 1970. A Guide to the Birds of South America. Wynnewood, Pennsylvania: Livingston Publishing Company. 470 pp.

Meyer de Schauensee, R., and W. H. Phelps, Jr. 1978. A Guide to the Birds of Venezuela. Princeton, New Jersey: Princeton University Press. 424 pp.

Morony, J. J., Jr., W. J. Bock, and J. Farrand, Jr. 1975. Reference List of the Birds of the World. New York: American Museum of Natural History, Department of Ornithology. 207 pp.

Murphy, R. C. 1925. Bird Islands of Peru. New York: G. P. Putnam's Sons. 362 pp.

Oficina Nacional de Evaluación de Recursos Naturales (ONERN). 1976. Mapa Ecológico del Perú: Guía Explicativa. Lima:ONERN. 146 pp.

O'Neill, J. P., and G. R. Graves. 1977. A new genus and species of owl (Aves: Strigidae) from Peru. Auk 94:409–416.

O'Neill, J. P., and D. L. Pearson. 1974. Estudio preliminar de las aves de Yarinacocha, Departamento de Loreto, Perú. Publicacion del Museo de Historia Natural "Javier Prado," Seria A (Zoologia) 25:1–13.

O'Neill, J. P., and M. A. Plenge. MS. A Guide to the Birds of the Paracas Peninsula Region.

Parker, T. A., III. 1976. Finding the Marvelous Spatuletail. Birding 8:175.

———. 1980. Birding the selva of southeastern Peru at Explorer's Inn. Birding 12:221–223.

Parker, T. A., III, and J. P. O'Neill. 1976a. An introduction to bird-finding in Peru: Part I. The Paracas Peninsula and Central Highway (Lima to Huanuco City). Birding 8:140–144.

———. 1976b. An introduction to bird-finding in Peru: Part II. The Carpish Pass Region of the Eastern Andes along the Central Highway. Birding 8:205–216.

———. 1980. Notes on little known birds of the upper Urubamba Valley, southern Peru. Auk 97:167–176.

———. 1981. An introduction to bird-finding in Peru: Part III. Tingo María and the Divisoria Mountains. Birding 13:100–106.

Paynter, R. A. (ed.). 1970. *In* J. L. Peters, Check-list of Birds of the World, Vol. XIII: Emberizinae, Catamblyrhynchinae, Cardinalinae, Thraupinae, Tersinae. Cambridge, Massachusetts: Museum of Comparative Zoology. 443 pp.

Phelps, W. H., Jr., and R. Meyer de Schauensee. 1979. Una Guia de las Aves de Venezuela. Caracas: Gráficas Armitanas C.A. 484 pp.

Richards, P. W. 1966. The Tropical Rain Forest: An Ecological Study. Cambridge, England: Cambridge University Press. 450 pp.

Short, L. L. 1975. A zoogeographic analysis of the South American chaco avifauna. American Museum of Natural History, Bulletin 154:163–352.

Stager, K. E. 1968. A new piculet from southeastern Peru. Los Angeles County Museum of Natural History, Contributions to Science No. 153:1–4.

Terborgh, J. W. MS. The birds and larger mammals of Cocha Cashu, Manu National Park.

Terborgh, J. W., and J. S. Weske. 1975. The role of competition in the distribution of Andean birds. Ecology 56:562–576.

Tosi, J. A. 1960. Zonas de Vida Natural en el Perú: Memoria Explicativa sobre el Mapa Ecológico del Perú. Instituto Interamericano de Ciencias Agrícolas de la OEA, Zona Andina, Proyecto 39, Programa de Cooperación Tecnica, Boletin Técnico No. 5. Washington, D.C.: Organización de Estados Americanos. 271 pp.

Traylor, M. (ed.) 1979. In J. L. Peters, Check-list of Birds of the World, Vol. VIII: Tyrannidae, Pipridae, Cotingidae, Oxyruncidae, Phytotomidae, Pittidae, Philepittidae, Acanthisittidae, Menuridae, Atrichornithidae. Cambridge, Massachusetts: Museum of Comparative Zoology. 365 pp.

Vaurie, C. 1971. Classification of the Ovenbirds (Furnariidae). London: H. F. & G. Witherby Ltd. 46 pp.

Weske, J. S., and J. W. Terborgh. 1974. *Hemispingus parodii*, a new species of tanager from Peru. Wilson Bulletin 86:97–103.

———. 1977. *Phaethornis koepckeae*, a new species of hummingbird from Perú. Condor 79:143–147.

———. 1981. *Otus marshalli*, a new species of screech-owl from Perú. Auk 98:1–7.

ADDITIONAL READING

Coker, R. E. 1920. Peru's wealth-producing birds. National Geographic Magazine 37:537–566.

George, W. G. 1964. Rarely seen songbirds of Peru's high Andes. Natural History 78(8):26–29.

Haverschmidt, F. 1968. Birds of Surinam. Edinburgh and London: Oliver and Boyd. 445 pp.

Hughes, R. A. 1972. The adjacent region of south-west Peru. In A. W. Johnson (ed.), Supplement to the Birds of Chile and Adjacent Regions of Argentina, Bolivia and Peru. Buenos Aires: Platt Establecimientos Gráficos, pp. 40–53.

———. 1976. Additional records of birds from the Mollendo district, coast of southwest Peru. Condor 78:118–119.

———. 1979. Notes on Charadriiformes of the south coast of Peru. In F. A. Pitelka (ed.), Shorebirds in Marine Environments. Studies in Avian Biology 2:49–53.

Morrison, A. 1939. The birds of the Department of Huancavelica, Peru. Ibis, Ser. 14, 3:453–486.

———. 1939. Notes on the birds of Lake Junin, central Peru. Ibis, Ser. 14, 3:643–654.

Murphy, R. C. 1924. The most valuable bird in the world. National Geographic Magazine 46:278–302.

———. 1927. The Peruvian guano islands seventy years ago. Natural History 27:439–447.

———. 1936. Oceanic Birds of South America. 2 vols. New York: MacMillan. 1245 pp.

———. 1959. Peru profits from sea fowl. National Geographic Magazine 115:395–413.

O'Neill, J. P. 1974. The Birds of Balta, a Peruvian Dry Tropical Forest Locality, with an Analysis of Their Origins and Ecological Relationships. Ph.D. Dissertation, Louisiana State University, Baton Rouge, Louisiana. 284 pp.

Paulik, G. J. 1971. Anchovies, birds, and fishermen in the Peru Current. In W. W. Murdoch (ed.), Environment, Resources, Pollution, and Society, pp. 156–185. Stamford, Connecticut: Sinauer Associates, Inc.

Pearson, D. L., and M. A. Plenge. 1974. Puna bird species on the coast of Peru. Auk 91:626–631.

Plenge, M. A. 1974. Notes on some birds in west-central Peru. Condor 76:326–330.

Ridgely, R. S. 1976. A Guide to the Birds of Panama. Princeton, New Jersey: Princeton University Press. 394 pp.

Roe, N. A., and W. E. Rees. 1979. Notes on the puna avifauna of Azángaro Province, Department of Puno, southern Peru. Auk 96:475–482.

Schaefer, M. B. 1970. Men, birds, and anchovies in the Peru Current — dynamic interactions. American Fisheries Society, Transactions 99:461–467.

Tallman, D. A. 1974. Colonization of a Semi-isolated Temperate Cloud Forest: Preliminary Interpretation of Distributional Patterns of Birds in the Carpish Region of the Department of Huánuco, Peru. M.S. Thesis, Louisiana State University, Baton Rouge, Louisiana. 148 pp.

Weske, J. S. 1972. The Distribution of the Avifauna in the Apurimac Valley of Peru with Respect to Environmental Gradients, Habitat, and Related Species. Ph.D. Dissertation, University of Oklahoma, Norman, Oklahoma. 137 pp.

INDEX TO COMMON NAMES*

The names of families appear in capital letters.

*Thanks to Norm and Maggie Mellor for providing the first version of this index.

INDEX TO GENERA

Metriopelia, 40
Micrastur, 34
Microbates, 71
Microcerculus, 70
Micromonacha, 48
Micropalama, 38
Micropygia, 36
Microrhopias, 56
Milvago, 35
Mimus, 70
Mionectes, 62
Mitrephanes, 65
Mitu, 35
Mniotilta, 72
Molothrus, 71
Momotus, 48
Monasa, 49
Morphnus, 34
Muscigralla, 66
Muscisaxicola, 66
Muscivora, 68
Myadestes, 70
Mycteria, 32
Myiarchus, 67
Myiobius, 64
Myioborus, 73
Myiodynastes, 67
Myiopagis, 61
Myiophobus, 64, 65
Myiornis, 63
Myiotheretes, 65, 66
Myiotriccus, 64
Myiozetetes, 67
Myospiza, 79
Myrmeciza, 57
Myrmia, 47
Myrmoborus, 57
Myrmochanes, 57
Myrmothera, 58
Myrmotherula, 56
Myrtis, 47

Nasica, 51
Nemosia, 76
Neochelidon, 69
Neochen, 32
Neocrex, 36
Neoctantes, 55
Neomorphus, 42

Neopelma, 60
Neopipo, 60
Nephelornis, 74
Netta, 33
Nonnula, 49
Notharchus, 48
Nothocercus, 29
Nothocrax, 35
Nothoprocta, 29
Nothura, 29
Notiochelidon, 68
Numenius, 38
Nuttallornis, 65
Nyctibius, 43
Nycticorax, 31
Nyctidromus, 43
Nyctiphrynus, 43
Nyctiprogne, 43
Nystalus, 48

Ochthoeca, 65
Ochthornis, 65
Oceanites, 30
Oceanodroma, 30
Ocreatus, 46
Ocyalus, 71
Odontophorus, 35
Odontorchilus, 69
Onychorhynchus, 64
Opisthocomus, 35
Opisthoprora, 47
Oporornis, 72
Oreomanes, 73
Oreonympha, 47
Oreopholus, 37
Oreotriccus, 61
Oreotrochilus, 46
Ornithion, 61
Oroaetus, 34
Ortalis, 35
Ortygonax, 36
Oryzoborus, 78
Otus, 42
Oxyruncus, 68
Oxyura, 33

Pachyptila, 30
Pachyramphus, 68
Pandion, 34

Panyptila, 44
Parabuteo, 34
Pardirallus, 36
Paroaria, 77
Parula, 72
Passer, 71
Patagona, 46
Pauxi, 35
Pelagodroma, 30
Pelecanoides, 31
Pelecanus, 31
Penelope, 35
Percnostola, 57
Petrochelidon, 69
Phacellodomus, 53, 54
Phaeomyias, 61
Phaeoprogne, 68
Phaeotriccus, 66
Phaethon, 31
Phaethornis, 44
Phaetusa, 39
Phalacrocorax, 31
Phalaropus, 38
Phalcoboenus, 35
Pharomachrus, 47
Phegornis, 37
Pheucticus, 77
Philomachus, 38
Philydor, 54
Phlegopsis, 57
Phleocryptes, 52
Phloeceastes, 50
Phlogophilus, 45
Phoenicircus, 59
Phoenicoparrus, 32
Phoenicopterus, 32
Phyllomyias, 61
Phylloscartes, 63
Phyrgilus, 78
Phytotoma, 68
Piaya, 42
Piculus, 50
Picumnus, 50
Piezorhina, 77
Pilherodius, 31
Pionites, 41
Pionopsitta, 41
Pionus, 41
Pipile, 35

Pipra, 60
Pipraeidea, 74
Pipreola, 59
Piprites, 60
Pipromorpha, 62
Piranga, 75
Pitangus, 67
Pithys, 57
Pitylus, 77
Platycichla, 70
Platypsaris, 68
Platyrinchus, 64
Plegadis, 32
Pluvialis, 37
Podager, 43
Podiceps, 29
Podilymbus, 30
Poecilotriccus, 63
Pogonotriccus, 63
Polioptila, 71
Polyborus, 35
Polyonymus, 46
Polyplancta, 45
Polytmus, 45
Poospiza, 79
Poospizopsis, 79
Popelairia, 45
Porphyriops, 36
Porphyrolaema, 59
Porphyrula, 36
Porzana, 36
Premnornis, 54
Premnoplex, 54
Procellaria, 30
Progne, 68
Psarocolius, 71
Pseudocolaptes, 54
Pseudocolopteryx, 62
Pseudotriccus, 63
Psophia, 36
Pterocnemia, 29
Pterodroma, 30
Pteroglossus, 49
Pterophanes, 46
Puffinus, 30
Pulsatrix, 42
Pygiptila, 55
Pyriglena, 57
Pyrocephalus, 65

Map. 3 Departments and principal cities of Peru.

RECENT ADDITIONS TO THE PERU LIST

*Pinnated Bittern — *Botaurus pinnatus*
*Southern Lapwing — *Vanellus chilensis*
*Rufous-necked Sandpiper — *Calidris ruficollis*
*Noble Snipe — *Gallinago nobilis*
White-chinned Thistletail — *Schizoeaca fuliginosa*
Vilcabamba Thistletail — *S. vilcabambae*
*Point-tailed Palmcreeper — *Berlepschia rikeri*
Short-billed Leafscraper — *Sclerurus rufigularis*
*Collared Gnatwren — *Microbates collaris*
Tangara — sp. nov.
White-bellied Seedeater — *Sporophila leucoptera*
*Bicolored Seedeater — *S. bicolor*